Cinderella

A Pantomime

Norman Robbins

Samuel French — London
New York — Sydney — Toronto — Hollywood

CHARACTERS

Dandini, squire to the Prince
Buttons, page to Baron Hardupp
Cinderella, the Baron's daughter
Baron Hardupp, of Stoneybroke Mansion
Baroness Hardupp, his new wife
Asphyxia
Euthanasia } her daughters
Ammer
Tongs } the broker's men
Prince Charming, of Castle Glamorous
Fairy Godmother
Major Domo
Villagers, Footmen, Huntsmen, Courtiers, Junior Misses
and **Sunbeams Chorus**

AUTHOR'S NOTE

As a pantomime subject, *Cinderella* needs no introduction from me or anyone else. Possibly the world's most famous fictional story, there can be very few places where *some* adaptation of it has not been seen.

This being the case, I have followed the accepted version of the legend (so far as pantomime goes) and have tried to keep it scaled down to a manageable size for any stage in the country.

The storyline remains uncluttered, the romantic interest strong, and above all, the comedy fast moving. I deliberately overwrote the roles of the Ugly Sisters, as I have no way of knowing if producing societies will use men or women for the parts, and trust individual directors to prune lines accordingly. However, with two *good* performers, it can be played (and has been, with devastating results) uncut.

Like all pantomimes, it should be played at a fairly rapid pace, and the faster the insults fly, the better. This helps point up the gentler scenes as they occur. Please select songs and music with care. If you wish to add more, there are plenty of opportunities, and should you want less, then adjust the script accordingly.

Finally, I hope you'll enjoy this version of "Cinders" as much as I did writing it.

Norman Robbins

For
Iris and Alf

ACT I

The Village of Merrivale

A typical pantomime village setting, with a backdrop of houses and dense woods. A high brick wall, in which is set the iron gates of Stoneybroke Mansion, is on one side, and part of the Mansion can be seen above the wall. Shops, houses and an Inn can be seen on the other side

When the CURTAIN *rises, it is morning, bright and sunny, and the Villagers are enjoying themselves with song and dance*

SONG 1

At the end of the routine, Dandini enters upstage, from the direction of the woods. The Villagers fall back as he moves down

Dandini (*cheerily*) Greetings, good people of Merrivale. I am Dandini, squire to His Royal Highness Prince Charming, and I bring you good news.

The Villagers react and move in closer

Today, His Royal Highness is hunting in yonder woods—(*he indicates them*)—and he cordially invites you all to join his party.

The Villagers cheer delightedly

Furthermore—he bids me tell you that should the hunt be a successful one, then a great Ball will be held at Castle Glamorous this very evening, so that all may celebrate with him.

The Villagers cheer again, and Dandini joins them in a reprise of the opening song before they all exit in high spirits

There is a slight pause, then Buttons is heard calling from the Mansion

Buttons (*off*) Cinderella. Cinderella.

Buttons rushes out through the gates of Stoneybroke Mansion, waving an envelope

Hey, Cinders . . . (*He looks around*) Oh, blimey. Where's she got to now? (*He calls*) Cinderella. (*To the audience*) I don't suppose *you* lot have seen her, have you? No—I didn't think you would have. Most of you haven't even finished unwrapping your chocolate boxes yet, have you? Oh—I know what goes on out there. You think we can't see you from up here with all the lights off—but we *can*, you know. We can see everything. I'll prove it to you, shall I? (*He points into the audience*) You see there? In the fifth row? There's a woman sitting with her knees up. (*He peers at the fifth row*) Oh—I'm ever so sorry. It's two bald men sitting with their heads close together. No—wait a minute. I'll think of something else. Yes—I know. Do you realize, that since the lights went out and that overture started—over sixty boxes of Maltesers, two hundred Mars Bars, a hundred and twenty tubes of Smarties, and fifty-three packets of Polo Mints have been eaten—by this little boy in the front row? (*He points*) No—I'm only joking. He's still got two Mars bars left. (*He chuckles*) Well, hello, boys and girls. My name's Buttons. (*He spells it*) B.U.—(*He pauses*)—Uttons. Buttons. And I'm a pageboy for Baron Hardupp in Stoneybroke Mansion. (*He laughs*) Stoneybroke Mansion. They couldn't have picked a better name for it, could they? Nobody's got any money. Not even the Baron. I haven't had any wages for the past ten years. And I have to do all the work, you know. Cooking, cleaning, washing, gardening—*and* the ironing. In fact that's what I've been doing this morning. Ironing the curtains in the bedrooms. I didn't make a very good job of 'em though. I kept falling out of the windows. And the *dust*. Well, you know what they say about dust, don't you? We come from it when we're born, and we go to it when we die. Well there's somebody either coming or going under those beds, I can tell you. Anyway—I can't stand here all day chatting to you, even if you *are* the best-looking audience we've had in all week, I've got to find Cinderella and tell her the good news about her dad. (*He realizes*) Oh—I didn't tell you about that, did I? No. Well—you see—Cinder-ella's the Baron's daughter, and she's ever so smashing. If you ask me, she's the prettiest girl in the whole wide world and—well—you won't tell anybody, will you? I'm in love with her. (*He squirms shyly*) Anyway —I've just got this letter for her (*he shows it*)—and it says that they're going to let her dad come home again. He's going to be *freed*. Oh, she isn't half going to be pleased when she hears about it. She cried and cried when he had to go in *there*. They wouldn't even let her go visit him without a pass, and she was terrified of all those big guard dogs. And it's not been very nice for her round here since he went. Well—you know what *some* folk can be like. All those nasty remarks. Still—he'd nobody to blame but himself. He would go to Butlins for his holidays. Ah well, I'd better start looking again, but if you *do* happen to see Cinders anywhere about, you will tell her I'm looking for her, won't you? Just say Buttons wants you and . . .

Dandini enters

(*Spotting him*) Aye aye. (*To Dandini*) Er—excuse me.
Dandini Yes?
Buttons I don't suppose *you've* seen Cinders, have you?
Dandini (*blankly*) I beg your pardon?
Buttons Cinders. Cinders.
Dandini (*turning away*) Not today, thank you.
Buttons (*to the audience*) Ohhhh—there's one in every village, isn't there?
(*To Dandini*) Hoy, Fancypants . . .

Dandini turns in surprise

I'm not *selling* Cinders. I'm *looking* for Cinders.

Dandini (*tartly*) Then I suggest you try searching through the local dustbins.

Buttons No, no. Not *ashes* cinders. Cinders from the Mansion. *Cinderella* Cinders. Baron Hardupp's daughter.

Dandini (*realizing*) Oh, I'm terribly sorry. I thought . . . Please forgive me.

Buttons Oh, that's all right. You can't help being stupid. Well? *Have* you seen her?

Dandini (*mustering a smile*) I'm sorry, but I'm a stranger to these parts. I'm afraid I wouldn't know her even if I had.

Buttons Oh, you would do. She's the most beautiful girl in the world, and as soon as I get rich enough I'm going to marry her.

Dandini Oh. Waiting for your ship to come in, are you?

Buttons Not half. The only trouble is, I've been waiting so long, the blooming pier's starting to collapse. So you haven't seen her then?

Dandini (*doubtfully*) I don't think so. You see—I only came to Merrivale to deliver a message from the Royal party.

Buttons Oh. That's funny—'cos *I'm* looking for Cinders to deliver a message to *her*. Her dad's coming back from Butlins today and he says he's got a big surprise for her.

Dandini How nice. Then he'll be just in time for the Ball at the Palace, if all goes well.

Buttons A Ball at the Palace?

Dandini This very night. I'll be around with the tickets later.

Buttons Here—can I come as well?

Dandini But of course. The Prince will invite *everyone*.

Buttons (*awed*) Cor. I've never been to a Ball at the Palace before. What will I have to wear?

Dandini (*amused*) Anything you like.

Buttons (*thinking quickly*) Well—the Baron *did* buy me a new outfit for my birthday—so I might as well wear *that*, eh?

Dandini You mean . . .?

Buttons Yeh. I'll come in my birthday suit.

Buttons exits into the Mansion

Dandini And *I'd* better be getting back to the Hunt. The Prince will be wondering where on earth I've got to.

Dandini exits towards the woods. As he does so, Cinderella enters from the Mansion in a shabby dress. She is singing

SONG 2

After the song she twirls round happily, her arms outstretched

Cinders What a *wonderful* day it is today. Not a cloud in the sky, and the first day of Spring. I don't mind being poor at all on a day like this. Oh, if only Daddy were here.

Baron (*off*) Cinderella. Cinderella. I'm home.

Baron Hardupp enters from the woods carrying a small suitcase

Cinders.

Cinders Daddy.

She rushes to him and they embrace

Baron Oh, it's good to be home again, my love. I've missed you so very much.

Cinders (*moving down with him*) And *I've* missed *you*, Daddy. Did you have a nice time?

Baron Oh, marvellous, my dear. Simply marvellous. I won the knobbliest knees competition two weeks running, and guess what *else*.

Cinders What?

Baron Our troubles are over. From now on, we'll have money to burn.

Cinders (*bewildered*) You mean—you've won some money?

Baron (*chuckling*) No, no, no, my dear. Something *much* better than that. I've got the most wonderful surprise for you. (*Rubbing his hands with glee*) I just know you're going to be thrilled. Now close your eyes for a moment, and you'll see. No peeping, mind.

Cinderella closes her eyes. The Baron signals off towards the woods

The Baroness enters, in a temper

Baroness (*fiercely*) What do you mean by keeping me waiting over there? (*She sees Cinders and shrieks in horror*) Aaaaaagh, what is it? Save me. (*She flings her arms around the Baron's neck*) Save me.

Cinders (*opening her eyes at the commotion*) What is it? What's wrong?

Baroness (*shrieking*) It spoke. It *spoke*. (*She clutches the Baron more tightly*) Mercy.

Baron (*flustered*) What is it, Medusa, my pet? What's *wrong*?

Baroness (*pointing at Cinders*) THAT! That MONSTER! (*She cowers*)

Baron But—but—that's my *daughter*.

Baroness (*in horror*) Daughter?

Baron Little Cinderella.

Baroness Oooooooooh. (*She collapses in a dead faint in his arms*)

Cinders (*scared*) What's wrong with her, Daddy? Why has she fainted?

Baron (*weakly*) It must have been the shock, my dear. I don't think she realized how *grown up* you were.

Cinders But she called me a *monster*. (*Anxiously*) Who is she?

Baron Well—er—she's your surprise.

Cinders What?

Baron (*uncomfortably*) I decided to get married again. She's your new stepmother.

Cinders (*aghast*) Oh, no.

Baron (*pleading*) She has money, my sweet, and you know how poor *we* are. The broker's men are coming today to throw us out of the Mansion unless we can pay our debts.

Baroness (*recovering fast*) Well if you think you're going to pay them off with *my* money, you've another think coming. Now *I'm* mistress of Stoneybroke Mansion, there's going to be a few changes around here— and for a start THAT—(*she points at Cinderella*)—is going to sleep in the kitchen.

Cinders and the Baron react

Baron Sleep in the kitchen? She most certainly *isn't*. Why should she?

Baroness Because with a face like hers, if ever we have burglars, she'll frighten them away. (*To Cinders*) Now get inside that house, you lazy little toad, and prepare the bedrooms for my two lovely daughters, Asphyxia and Euthanasia.

Baron (*startled*) Daughters? I didn't know you had any *daughters*.

Baroness (*snapping*) Well you know now, so get cracking and do as I tell you to, or you'll never see a penny of my money. (*She marches to the gates*) I'm off to see what the rest of this crumbling old dump looks like.

The Baroness exits into the Mansion

Cinders Oh Daddy. She's *awful*.

Baron (*sadly*) I'm sorry, Cinders. (*He puts his arm round her*) I was only trying to do what I thought was best. It looks as though I was wrong after all.

The Baron and Cinders exit slowly into the Mansion. As they do so, Asphyxia and Euthanasia enter from the woods in outrageous gowns

Asphyxia (*teetering downstage*) Yoo-hoo. Mummy. (*She peers around*)

Euthanasia (*mincing after her*) We're here. (*Scornfully*) Cor, what a dump. Look at that great pile of rubbish over there. (*She points at a shop*)

Asphyxia (*drily*) That's your reflection in the shop window. I wonder where Mumsy's got to?

Euthanasia Who cares? She's probably knocking back the gin in the— (*local pub*)—by this time. Drunken old cat.

Asphyxia Well, dear (*She wanders round*) there's one thing to be said for living in a flea pit like this. I'll be the most attractive young thing in the area. (*She simpers*)

Euthanasia (*scornfully*) Hah. You mean *I* will, don't you, ducky?

Asphyxia You? (*Turning to her*) Listen, prune-features. You won't stand a chance when the boys get an eyeful of *this* figure. I'll just give 'em one of my famous "come hither" looks—

Euthanasia And they'll run for their lives.

Asphyxia (*ignoring this*)—Pucker my lips like this . . . (*She does so*)

Euthanasia And *they'll* hold their stomachs like *this*. (*She clutches her stomach as though she is about to be sick*)

Asphyxia (*sweetly*) Careful, dahling—or I'll fill your face in for you. (*She preens*) It has been said that *my* face is the exact image of Helen of Troy's . . .

Euthanasia Three thousand years after they buried her.

Asphyxia (*firmly*) And *her* face launched a thousand ships. (*She glares*)

Euthanasia I'm not surprised. If she'd a clock half as ugly as yours is, they'd have been launched to escape from the sight of it.

Asphyxia (*snarling*) You've some need to talk, you grotty looking old ragbag. I've a good mind to smack you right in the middle of those fat, flabby chops.

Euthanasia (*sneering*) Huh. You know what *your* trouble is, don't you? (*She turns away*) You're jealous of my beauty.

Asphyxia *Beauty?* (*She shrieks with laughter*) If I had a face like yours, I'd put it on a wall and throw a brick at it.

Euthanasia And if I had a face like *yours*, I'd put it on a brick and throw a *wall* at it.

Asphyxia Is that so? Well, let me tell you, slugface—*I've* had songs written about my beauty.

Euthanasia Oh, I know. I've *heard* one of them. *The Hippopotamus Song.* (*She sings*) "mud, mud, glorious mud".

Asphyxia rushes at her, handbag flying.

Euthanasia defends herself, screeching loudly

Buttons enters from the Mansion

Buttons (*spotting them*) Oo-er.

Asphyxia
Euthanasia } A MAN! } (*Speaking together*)

They break apart and quickly tidy themselves

Asphyxia He's mine. (*She flings her sister to one side*)

Euthanasia (*recovering*) Oh, no he's not. I saw him first. (*She grabs hold of Asphyxia and pulls her back*)

Asphyxia (*struggling*) Let go, you foul faced-cat.

Euthanasia (*tugging*) He's mine, I tell you. Mine.

Asphyxia (*lashing out with her handbag again*) Take that.

Euthanasia (*as the bag makes contact*) Owww!

Buttons (*gaping*) Blimey. I'd better go phone the Zoo and tell 'em that two have escaped.

The Baroness, Baron and Cinders enter

Baroness (*to the sisters*) What is it, my poppets? What's happening?

Euthanasia She hit me. (*She points at her sister*)

Asphyxia (*astounded*) I didn't. It was him. (*She points at Buttons*)

Buttons (*stunned*) It was *me*?

Asphyxia (*triumphantly*) You see, Mama. He *admits* it. The brute.

Baroness (*turning on Buttons*) How dare you attack my little Euthanasia?

Buttons I never touched the ugly old faggot (*to the audience*) did I, kids? (*After the audience reacts*) See?

Euthanasia Yes you did, you pint-sized little ... (*She spots Cinderella*) And what's *that*?

Asphyxia (*peering at Cinders in awe*) Is it *real*?

Baron (*putting his arms round Cinders protectively*) This is your little stepsister, Cinderella.

Euthanasia (*aghast*) Stepsister? *That* scruffy-looking object my *stepsister*? Oh, it's not *true*. It *can't* be true.

Asphyxia (*reeling in anguish*) I feel faint. I don't *believe* it. How can someone as lovely as *me* have a dreadful looking thing like that for a *stepsister*?

Baroness I know. She's too ghastly for words, my sweets, but don't worry yourselves. I'll make quite sure she keeps her ugly face hidden when we have visitors. We can always lock her in the cellar, can't we?

Buttons Stop picking on Cinders, you ugly old witches. She's worth a hundred of *you lot*.

Baroness (*to Buttons*) How dare you speak to us like that? Leave the Mansion at once. You're fired.

Cinderella Oh, no. Please don't send Buttons away. He's the only friend I've got.

Asphyxia (*savagely mocking*) "Please don't send Buttons away. He's the only friend I've got". (*She snarls*) Well I've got news for you, ducky. You've just *lost* him.

Cinders (*to the Baron*) *Do* something, Daddy.

Baron Of course I will. (*To the Baroness*) Now just you look here . . .

Baroness (*snapping*) You shut your cakehole. *I'll* give the orders from now on. Remember?

Cinders (*pleading*) Oh, please let Buttons stay.

Buttons Don't worry, Cinders. I'll soon find another job. I wouldn't stay here and serve them, anyway. *I'm* used to better things.

Asphyxia And what do you mean by *that* remark? Let me tell you, *we* move in the very best of circles, don't we, Sister?

Euthanasia We certainly do. There isn't a month goes by without *us* appearing at Court. (*She preens herself*)

Buttons Yes—the *Magistrate's* Court. The nearest *you two* have ever been to Royalty is when you've been drinking tea out of a Coronation mug.

Baroness Ignore him, my angels. We'd better get the things into the house.

Baron Things? What things?

Asphyxia (*sweetly*) Why—just the few things we've been buying in the town, Daddy dear. (*She gives him a huge false smile*)

Euthanasia (*calling off*) Bring 'em in, boys.

Several footmen enter, staggering under the mountains of gift-wrapped packages. They line up, as the Baron gazes at them in horror

Baron But—but—but . . .

Asphyxia Now don't worry, Popsie. We've got something for you too.

Euthanasia Of course we have. (*She produces a slip of paper*) The bill. (*She stuffs it in his top pocket*)

Euthanasia exits through the Mansion gates, followed by the Baroness, Asphyxia and Footmen

Baron (*weakly*) I'm ruined. Ruined.

The Baron totters off after the others

Cinders (*almost in tears*) Oh, Buttons. Whatever are we going to do? They're horrible. Absolutely horrible. (*She breaks down and sobs*) I wish I were dead.

Buttons (*worried*) Here—you mustn't say things like that, Cinders. What would *I* do if you went and died?

Cinders (*trying to smile*) Would you miss me, Buttons? Honest?

Buttons Miss you? I'll say I'd miss you. I wouldn't have anybody to darn me socks for me, would I?

Cinders (*laughing despite herself*) Buttons!

Buttons And anyway—if you were dead—you wouldn't be able to go to the Ball tonight, would you?

Cinders A Ball? Tonight? But *where*?

Buttons (*pleased*) Ah, that's got you interested, hasn't it? It's at Castle Glamorous, and everybody in the village has been invited.

Cinders (*delighted*) Oh, I can't believe it. How did you find out?

Buttons Oh, some fancy-looking feller wearing lipstick, high heels and no trousers told me.

Cinders (*as the thought strikes her*) But what's the use in telling us? We can't even afford to change our minds, let alone go to a Ball.

Buttons Ah, but that's the *best* bit. It's all free. Anybody can go. He's going to bring the tickets round later.

Cinders (*brightening again*) Oh, Buttons. That's *marvellous*. (*She hugs him*)

Buttons (*happily*) That's better. You're laughing again.

Cinders Thanks to you. (*She breaks free*) Oh, I must go and tell Daddy. (*She gives him a quick kiss*) I love you, Buttons.

Cinders exits to the Mansion

Buttons (*dazed*) She loves me. Did you hear that, kids? She loves me.

SONG 3

After the song, Buttons exits into the Mansion. As he does so, Ammer and Tongs enter from the woods

Ammer Well—here we are, Mr Tongs. Stoneybroke Mansion. In you go. (*He indicates the gateway*)

Tongs Right you are, Mr Ammer. (*He begins to move, then stops and turns back*) Just a minute. Just a *minute*. What do you mean—in you go? What are *you* going to do?

Ammer What do you *think* I'm going to do? I'm going to stand here and count the things as you throw them out, aren't I?

Tongs Oh. I never thought of that. I'll go right inside then.

Tongs exits into the Mansion. A moment later, he yells loudly and comes flying out again to land in a heap at Ammer's feet

Ammer (*counting*) One.

Tongs (*picking himself up painfully*) Here, I say . . .

Ammer (*seeing him*) What are you doing down there? I thought I told you to go inside and start throwing the things out?

Tongs Yes, you did. But I . . .

Ammer Never mind the "buts". Get into that building and start earning your wages.

Tongs (*grumbling as he goes*) It's all right for you.

Tongs exits. There is a loud scream off and he comes hurtling out of the gates again, landing at Ammer's feet once more

Ammer (*counting*) One. (*He looks down*) Look—if you're going to play about on the floor all day, we're never going to get finished. Now stop messing about and *move* yourself.

Tongs (*getting up*) Look—why don't *you* go in and get the things, and *I'll* stand out here and count?

Ammer Oh, all right. Anything if it'll get us finished quicker.

Ammer exits into the Mansion

Tongs (*to the audience*) Watch this. (*He laughs*)

Ammer comes out with a chair, places it downstage, then turns to go back into the Mansion

Hey—Ammer. Just a minute.

Ammer (*turning*) Yes?

Tongs (*puzzled*) Is everything all right?

Ammer Why shouldn't it be?

Tongs I mean—didn't anything *happen* to you?

Ammer Like what?

Tongs Well—like—somebody picking you up and throwing you.

Ammer What *are* you talking about?

Tongs Oh, nothing. Look—*I'll* get the next chair, shall I?

Tongs exits into the Mansion. A yell, and he comes hurtling out again, to crash to the floor

Owww!

The Baroness comes striding out of the gates

Baroness And this time, STAY OUT! If I catch you round here again, I'll set the dogs on to you!

Ammer Who are *you*?

Baroness Baroness Hardupp, that's who I am, and from now on, *I'll* be giving the orders.

Tongs Right. We'll have two pints of beer and a cheese sandwich each.

Baroness Silence, you lanky layabout. Now clear off before I lose my temper.

Ammer Come on, Tongs. We'd better beat a retreat like the old battleaxe says.

Baroness *Old battleaxe?* How *dare* you? I happen to be a professional model, for your information.

Tongs Professional model? What for? Shipbuilders?

Baroness (*indignantly*) Oh. (*She screeches*) Asphyxia. Euthanasia.

The Sisters enter from the Mansion

10   Cinderella

Asphyxia What is it? (*She sees the men*) Oh—it *isn't*.
Euthanasia It *is*.
Together Laurel and Hardy.
Asphyxia (*to the Baroness*) What do they want, Mummy?
Ammer I'll *tell* you what we want. We want some rent money and if we
don't get it, we propose . . .
Asphyxia ⎱ We accept. ⎰ (*Speaking together*)
Euthanasia ⎰   ⎱

Each Sister grabs a man

Ammer (*struggling*) Gerroff.
Tongs Help. (*He breaks free and moves away*)
Euthanasia (*simpering*) Oh, they're *shy*. Our beauty's knocked 'em for six.
(*She flutters her lashes at Tongs*)
Ammer (*breaking free*) We want to collect the rent money, that's all, and
if it's not forthcoming, we've got strict orders to take you . . .
Asphyxia ⎱ Oh, take us ⎰ (*Speaking together*)
Euthanasia ⎰   ⎱

They each grab a man again. The men shriek with fear and fight free

Ammer and Tongs exit as quickly as possible

Asphyxia That's what I like. A bit of spirit. After them.
Euthanasia Tally-ho.

*The Sisters charge off in pursuit. As they do so, the Baron enters from the
Mansion*

Baron (*excitedly*) Medusa. Medusa, my love.
Baroness (*tartly*) And what do *you* want, sheep's-head?
Baron I've just been told that the Prince is hunting in the woods today,
and if the hunt is a good one, he'll be throwing a Ball at the Castle
tonight.
Baroness And what's so exciting about *that*? A grown man throwing a
ball at the Castle. What happens if he smashes a window with it, eh?
It's our rates that'll have to pay for a new one.
Baron No, no, my pet. You misunderstand. I mean a Ball *dance*. Everyone
in the Kingdom will be there.
Baroness (*realizing*) What? Oh—I must tell my little poppets at once. A
dance at the Castle. The perfect opportunity for them to trap some poor
idiot into proposing to them—I mean—to find themselves husbands.
Baron But only if the hunt is a good one, remember.
Baroness It *will* be. Phone—(*a local butcher's shop*)—at once and order
two thousand pheasants and a couple of hundred rabbits to be dumped
in the woods. We've got to have that Ball if it's the last thing we do. Now
hurry. (*Calling*) Asphyxiaaaa—Euthanasiaaaa . . .!

*The Baroness exits hurriedly after the Sisters and the Baron exits into the
Mansion as—*

the CURTAIN *falls*

SCENE 2

A Path in the Woods

Dance of the Sunbeams dressed as "Game". After the dance——

SONG 4 3

The Dancers exit, and Cinders enters, collecting sticks for the fire

Cinders How peaceful it is here in the woods. I could stay forever just listening to the song of the birds.

Buttons (*off*) Cinders? Cinders?

Buttons enters

Oh, *there* you are. I've been looking all over for you. Didn't you hear me calling?

Cinders (*muffled*) Hello, Buttons. (*She picks up more sticks*)

Buttons (*puzzled*) Something wrong? (*He moves round to look at her face*) Hey—you've been crying.

Cinders (*fighting back tears*) No, I haven't.

Buttons Yes you *have*. What's the matter? Have the Gruesome Twosome been bothering you again?

Cinders (*nodding*) Oh Buttons. I feel so miserable.

Buttons (*putting his arm round her*) Oh, come on, Cinders. Cheer up. You're not usually like this.

Cinders breaks down and cries

(*Gently*) Is there anything *I* can do to help?

Cinders (*shaking her head*) No. Just—just leave me alone for a while. I'll get over it. (*She pulls away from him*)

Buttons You mean—you want me to go away?

Cinders (*sniffling*) Please.

Buttons (*helplessly*) Oh.

He watches her, concerned, as she tries to stop her tears, then moves slowly away from her for a few steps

Cinders . . .

Cinders (*muffled*) Yes?

Buttons I *will* go away if you *really* want me to—but you *don't*, do you? Not *honestly*.

Cinders (*pulling herself together*) No, Buttons. Of course I don't.

Buttons (*hurrying back*) So what's wrong then? Oh, come on, Cinders. You can tell *me*.

Cinders (*wiping away her tears*) They won't let me go to the Ball tonight. My new stepmother and stepsisters.

Buttons (*scornfully*) Huh. They can't stop you. Old fancypants said anybody could go—even me. Now blow your nose and cheer up. Come on. (*He hands her his handkerchief*)

Cinders blows hard into it, then hands it back. He holds it up open to show a huge hole in the centre of it

Blimey. (*He stuffs it back in his pocket*)

Cinders But you don't understand, Buttons. My stepmother's been all round the village to tell everyone I won't be going, so they're all sending their children to the Mansion for me to look after. (*Sadly*) Oh, Buttons. I did *so* want to go to the Ball.

Buttons (*firmly*) Well, don't you worry, Cinders. You'll go to the Ball all right. *I'll* stay home and look after the kiddies.

Cinders (*delighted*) You will? (*Suddenly dejected again*) No. It wouldn't be fair.

Buttons I don't mind. Honest, I don't. I can't dance, anyway.

Cinders But what about a ticket? I haven't got one. They sent me out to gather sticks for the fire so that when the invitations came, I wouldn't be there to get one.

Buttons That's simple. You can have mine. I mean—*I* won't be needing it, will I?

Cinders (*overcome*) Oh, Buttons. I love you. (*She flings her arms round him*)

Buttons (*dazed*) She said it again.

Cinders If there's anything I can ever do for you . . .

Buttons Well—there is.

Cinders What is it?

Buttons Well—seeing as I'm not going to the Ball after all—and I don't even know how to dance—well—will you teach me, Cinders? Just for fun.

Cinders (*laughing*) Of course I will. In fact, I'll teach you right now.

Easy 2 sing (Salad Days)

SONG 5 4

And now I'd better finish gathering the sticks or I'll never be ready in time.

Cinders blows Buttons a kiss, and exits

Buttons (*calling*) Cinders. Wait. I'll give you a hand.

Buttons exits after Cinders

SONG 5

SCENE 3

A Woodland Glade We're throwing a ball tonight (Cole Porter)

Hunting Chorus (SONG 6), and possibly a ballet of Fox and Hounds. After the routine, Dandini enters

Dandini Make way for His Royal Highness, Prince Charming.

Huntsmen (*cheering*) Hooray!

Prince Charming enters

Prince (*brightly*) Thank you, my friends. Well, Dandini—it seems we shall be having our Ball this evening after all. Hunting is *extraordinarily* good today. Two thousand pheasants and a couple of hundred rabbits in a matter of only half-an-hour. It really *is* amazing. However there is *one* thing that puzzles me.

Dandini Sire?

Prince They all appear to be *pricemarked*. (*He holds up a rabbit*)

Dandini (*taken aback*) Good heavens!

Prince (*laughing*) Dandini, you old rogue. I suppose this is *your* doing?

Dandini I assure you . . .

Prince (*still amused*) I never thought you'd go to *these* lengths just for a dance. (*He coughs delicately*) I suppose they *are* all charged to me?

Dandini But I know nothing about it, Your Highness.

Prince (*puzzled*) Then—where did they come from?

Dandini I haven't the faintest idea.

Prince Oh, well—I've never been one to look a gift horse in the mouth. (*To the Huntsmen*) Take them all to the Castle and have the cooks prepare them for this evening.

The Huntsmen bow and exit.

Dandini Your Highness looks tired. Would you care to rest awhile in the shade of yonder tree?

Prince Oh, Dandini. If only you knew how much. The responsibilities of a prince are like a millstone round one's neck.

Dandini (*jesting*) I wouldn't mind having a millstone like that around *mine*. What *fun* I'd have in *your* place.

Prince (*smiling*) You think so?

Dandini I certainly do.

Prince (*clapping Dandini's shoulder*) Well, Dandini—I must admit that *I* envy *you*, too. If I were in your shoes for a while, and as free as the wind, you could bet your life I'd be having a fine old time with all those pretty village girls of yours.

Dandini Then why not . . . (*He breaks off and turns away*)

Prince Why not *what*?

Dandini (*uncomfortably*) Oh, nothing. It was just a sudden thought.

Prince Then tell me.

Dandini Well—why don't we *change places*? (*He turns to face the Prince*) Just for a while. You could be Dandini—and I could be His Royal Highness Prince Charming.

Prince (*laughing with glee*) Dandini, we couldn't. (*He thinks*) Could we?

Dandini We could give it a *try*.

Prince And we *shall*. Off with your coat.

With much amusement, they change coats and hats. When they finish dressing, the Prince laughs with delight

Voilà. (*He holds his arms out wide*) How do I look, Dandini?

Dandini (*haughtily*) I beg your pardon? *Prince Charming* to *you*—Dandini.

Prince (*laughing and bowing low*) I'm so sorry, Your Highness.

They both burst into laughter

Baron and Baroness Hardupp enter

Baroness (*spotting them*) Look. It's the Prince. Quick. Introduce me. (*She fusses about tidying herself*)

Baron (*flustered*) But what shall I say, my sweet?

Baroness "This is my wife", you idiot. (*She pushes the Baron forward*)

Baron (*coughing to attract attention*) Ahem.

The Prince and Dandini turn to him

Er . . . (*He indicates the Baroness*) This is my wife, you idiot.

Baroness (*shrieking*) Fool! *Fool!*

Baron (*hurriedly correcting himself*) I meant, this is my wife, you *fool*.

Prince (*sternly*) Who are you, insolent fellow?

Baron (*gulping*) Baron Hardupp of Stoneybroke Mansion, sir.

Baroness (*pushing herself forward*) And I'm his gracious wife, the Baroness Medusa Hardupp. (*She curtsies*)

Dandini (*frowning*) What do you want?

Baroness We've come to join the hunt, Your Highness.

Prince I'm afraid the hunt is over, madam. Everyone has gone back to Castle Glamorous to prepare for the Ball.

Dandini And the Prince—I mean *I* feel rather tired, so if you'll please excuse us . . .

Baron (*quickly*) Oh—er—yes. Of course. Certainly. At once. (*He bows, nods, curtsies, and turns round in confusion*)

Dandini and the Prince move away

Baroness (*elbowing the Baron*) *Tell* him.

Baron (*puzzled*) Tell him what?

Baroness (*hissing*) About my *daughters*.

Baron Why? He's done nothing wrong to you.

Baroness (*pushing him aside and calling*) Your Princefulship. Wait.

Prince } (*turning*) Yes? } (*Speaking together*)
Dandini }

The Prince remembers and turns away quickly

Baroness I'd like to introduce you to my two lovely daughters, Asphyxia and Euthanasia.

Dandini Oh—er—yes. Well—I'm sure I'll meet them at the Ball tonight. Please don't bother them now.

Baroness Oh, it's no bother. I'll just give them a little call. (*She bellows off*) Asphyxiaaaa! Euthanasiaaaa!

The Sisters enter, in hunting gear

Asphyxia (*spotting the Prince, as she thinks*) Oh, it's him. Prince Chow Mein.

Euthanasia (*screeching*) He's *mine*. (*She makes a dash for Dandini*)

Asphyxia (*grabbing her*) Not so fast, squint-eyes. Make one move in his direction, and I'll knock your teeth down your throat.

Euthanasia (*tugging free*) One more word from you, fish-face, and I'll sling *yours* in the river.

Baroness Girls, girls. (*She beams at them*) Such high spirits. Now come along and say hello to Princey.

Asphyxia (*simpering*) Hello, chuck. I'm Asphyxia, but *you* can call me Aspy. (*She curtsies, but falls over as Euthanasia pushes her*)

Euthanasia (*sickly sweet*) And *I'm* Euthanasia, but *you* can call me any time.

Euthanasia curtsies. Asphyxia kicks her over from the floor

Owwww!

Dandini (*shaken*) Pleased to meet you, I'm sure.

The Prince is doubled up with laughter

Asphyxia (*scrambling to her feet*) And what's *he* laughing at, may I ask?

Dandini Oh—er . . . He's thinking up jokes for the Ball tonight.

Euthanasia (*getting up*) He wants to try looking in a mirror.

Prince (*dropping his hat with shock*) I *beg* your pardon?

Asphyxia You heard.

Baroness (*to Dandini quickly*) We can't tell you how much we've enjoyed meeting you, Your Highjesty. Or how much we're looking forward to the Ball. As a matter of fact—we—er—we wondered if you might be wanting a little entertainment for the guests this evening?

Dandini Entertainment?

Baroness Why, yes. Asphyxia sings like a bird . . .

Euthanasia A crow. (*She smirks at Asphyxia*)

Baroness And Euthanasia can dance like a feather.

Asphyxia In an oil slick. (*She smirks at Euthanasia*)

Baroness I know they'd be only too *pleased* to perform for you tonight. (*To the girls*) Wouldn't you, my poppets?

Baron Well—that should take care of the *comedy* side of things.

Baroness (*throwing him a filthy look*) Why not show his Princefulness a little sample, darlings?

Dandini (*quickly*) Oh, no—I—please . . .

Euthanasia launches herself into a dreadful travesty of a dance: flat-footed, graceless and out of step, and all the while, a ghastly smile shows on a dead-pan face

Asphyxia (*to the audience*) Well, I'll say this much for her dancing. If she's got any enemies sitting out there, I reckon she's getting even with 'em. (*To Euthanasia*) Out of the way, duck-feet. It's time to show 'em some talent.

Euthanasia stops dancing and glares at her

Thank you. (*To the others*) Now *I'd* like to sing for you a little song that's going to haunt you for the rest of your lives.

Euthanasia Yes. *She's* going to murder it.

Asphyxia (*snapping*) I'll murder you in a minute, you glass-eyed toad. Now shut your great cavern while I enchant 'em with me vocalizing.

Euthanasia Vocalizing? You call that vocalizing? It's more like mutiny on the High Cs.

Asphyxia Is that so? Well let me tell you, ducky, there are folks sitting not more than five miles away from here who think I should be singing with Caruso.

Euthanasia I'm not surprised. He's been *dead* for years.

Asphyxia (*giving her a glare*) Ladies, Gentlemen—and OTHERS. (*She glowers at her sister*) Musetta's Waltz Song from *La Bohème*. (*She takes a deep breath and launches into the song. Loud, flat and out of tune*) "As through the streets—I wander onwards si-hing-ing . . ."

Euthanasia (*to the same tune*) They run her in for loitering.

Dandini (*interrupting the threatened punch-up*) Thank you. Thank you. We—er—we'll let you know.

Baroness Wasn't it *wonderful*?

Baron Yes. Especially when she stopped.

Dandini Well—I must confess I've never heard anything like it before.

Asphyxia That's because I've got a voice like an angel's.

Euthanasia Yes. It's like nothing on earth.

Prince (*moving in*) Dandi . . . I mean—Your Highness. Isn't it time we were getting back to the Castle?

Dandini Oh—er—yes. (*Eagerly*) Yes, of course. (*To the others*) Please excuse us.

Baroness Of course. (*She simpers*)

Dandini Good-bye.

Asphyxia Not good-bye, sweety-pie. Our Reservoir.

Dandini and the Prince quickly exit

Baroness (*delighted*) We've done it. We've done it.

Baron Done what?

Baroness Made a hit with the Prince, you dolt.

Asphyxia Well, I know *I* did. Did you see the look he gave me? It was love at first sight.

Euthanasia It looked more like *indigestion* to *me*.

Asphyxia Nobody's asking you, fishface. When I'm the Prince's bride, the first thing *I'm* going to do is to get rid of you.

Euthanasia Huh. The only bride you'll ever be is the Bride of Frankenstein.

Asphyxia (*stung*) If you open that branmasher of yours once more, I'll tear that greasy blonde hair out by its dirty black roots.

Euthanasia (*screeching*) Ooooh!

Baroness Girls, girls. Control yourselves. There's no need to fight over him.

Euthanasia It's all right for you. You managed to trap yourself a man. (*She glares at the Baron*) Loosely speaking. If we're not careful, we're going to be left on the shelf.

Baroness (*firmly*) Nonsense. When we get to the Ball tonight, there'll be plenty of men to choose from. Oh—I can see it all now. The tables loaded with food. The chandeliers loaded with candles. The men loaded with money.

Baron And you three loaded with gin.

Baroness ⎫
Asphyxia ⎬ What? ⎬ (*Speaking together*)
Euthanasia ⎭

All turn and chase the Baron off. Cinders enters with a bundle of sticks

Cinders I'll soon have finished now. Just a few more and then I can go. (*She picks up more sticks*)

An Old Lady enters, leaning on a staff

Old Lady (*in a quavery voice*) Excuse me, my child.

Cinders (*turning*) Oh. It's an old lady.

Old Lady Please help me gather a few sticks for my fire. These old bones of mine are not as supple as they used to be.

Cinders (*kindly*) Here. Take mine. (*She holds out her bundle*) I can easily gather more.

Old Lady (*protesting*) No, no. I couldn't possibly.

Cinders (*smiling*) Of course you could. (*She presses them into the Old Lady's arms*) Please. Now hurry home. It will soon be evening and the woods are no place for an elderly person. You could trip on a tree root and hurt yourself.

Old Lady (*backing away*) Thank you, my child. You are very kind to an old lady, and shall be rewarded for this unselfish act.

Cinders I don't want a reward. I'm only too pleased to be able to help.

Old Lady Nevertheless you shall have your reward just the same. When the time comes that you feel saddest, I shall come to your aid.

Cinders Well—it's very kind of you—but what can *you* do to help me?

Old Lady We shall see. We shall see.

The Old Lady exits slowly

Cinders What a strange old lady. And now I'd better start gathering more sticks. (*She sees the Prince's hat*) Oh. (*She picks it up*)

Prince Charming enters, searching

Prince (*to himself*) I must have dropped it somewhere around *here*. (*He sees Cinderella*) Oh—you've found it.

Cinders (*smiling*) Yours? (*She holds out the hat*)

Prince (*smiling*) I'm afraid I left here a few minutes ago in rather a hurry. (*He takes the hat from her*) Thank you, for rescuing it. (*He frowns*) Haven't I seen you somewhere before?

Cinders I don't think so, sir. I'm only a girl from the village.

Prince Strange. I seem to know your face.

Cinders Perhaps it's my father you know. Baron Hardupp.

Prince Baron Hardupp? Of Stoneybroke Mansion? I don't *believe* it.

Cinders Do you know Daddy, then?

Prince I'll say I know him. (*Amazed*) Do you mean to tell me that a beautiful girl like you is the sister of those two ugly-looking... (*He remembers*) Oh, I'm so sorry. I shouldn't have said that. Please forgive me.

Cinders Of course. It's not their fault they're like that, I suppose, but as a matter of fact, they're my stepsisters, not my real ones. My mother died when I was very small, and I'm an only child.

Prince What's your name?

Cinders Cinderella. What's yours?

Prince I am Prince Charming ... (*remembering*) 's valet, Dandini.

Cinders (*dreamily*) Dandini. What a lovely name.

Prince (*put out*) It's not as nice as Prince Charming, though.

Cinders Oh, yes it is. To me. I think it's the loveliest name I've ever heard.

Prince (*airily*) Of course, you haven't met the Prince yet, have you? Now *there's* a fine figure of a man.

Cinders (*shyly*) If he's as handsome as you are, then he must be.

Prince Oh, he's far more handsome than I. Wait till you see him at the Ball tonight. (*Anxiously*) You are coming to the Ball, aren't you?

Cinders Oh, yes.

Prince Then you must promise you'll dance with no-one but me all evening.

Cinders (*worried*) But what if the Prince should ...

Prince Pooh. Don't worry about *him*. He'll do just as I tell him to.

Cinders I must be dreaming.

Prince (*snapping his fingers*) That's it. That's where I've seen you before. In my dreams.

Cinders (*laughing*) Silly. Why should a fine gentleman like you dream about a poor girl like me?

Prince But it's true. I met you years ago in my dreams and we danced together on a carpet of clouds in a Palace of Crystal. You *must* remember. Say you remember.

Cinders If it will make you happy—I remember.

I know you
(Disney)

SONG 7 6

After the song, Buttons enters with more sticks

Buttons Oh, there you are, Cinders. I've gathered all these sticks for you and ... (*He sees the Prince*) Here—who's this, then?

Cinders This is Dandini, Buttons. He's the Prince's squire.

Buttons Prince's choir? Well let's hear him sing something then.

Prince (*laughing*) No, no. I can't sing.

Buttons I know. I was standing behind that tree listening to you.

Cinders (*excitedly*) Oh, Buttons. I'm going to dance every dance with him at the Ball tonight.

Buttons (*peeved*) Oh, are you? And what am I supposed to do, then?

Cinders (*surprised*) But—you said you'd stay at home and look after the village children for me.

Buttons Yes, I know. But I'm not going to if you're going to dance all night with *him*.

Cinders (*baffled*) But why?

Buttons And I shan't give you my ticket to go with, either.

Cinders Buttons!

Prince Don't worry, Cinderella. *I've* got plenty of tickets. (*He gives her one*) And now I'll really have to be going, but I'll be waiting for you tonight at the Castle. Farewell.

The Prince exits

Cinders Buttons. I'm ashamed of you. You were very rude to Dandini.

Buttons (*pouting*) Don't care.

Cinders It was very wrong of you.

Buttons (*crestfallen*) I'm sorry, Cinders. It's just that I can't bear to see anybody else with their arms round you.

Cinders Buttons. You're *jealous*.

Buttons (*squirming*) Well . . .

Cinders (*gently*) There's no need to be jealous, Buttons. I still like you, too.

Buttons You said you *loved* me.

Cinders And I do—

Buttons gives a happy grin

—as a brother.

He slumps again

Oh, Buttons. Please don't be upset. I'll always be a friend to you—honestly. But this is something different. I think I'm in love.

Buttons Huh.

Cinders Aren't you pleased for me, Buttons? Just a little?

Buttons No. (*He scuffs his shoe on the ground*)

Cinders (*slipping her arm around his shoulders*) Buttons?

Sulkily, he pulls away and moves away from her

(*Helplessly*) Well—I suppose I'd better be getting back to the Mansion.

Buttons (*still upset*) That's what I came to tell you. That new stepmother of yours is out looking for you.

Cinders What? Oh, dear. I'd better hurry, then. 'Bye, Buttons—and please cheer up.

Cinders exits quickly

Buttons (*calling after her*) I won't tell you the good news, now. I've got me old job back. (*To himself*) Huh, *she* doesn't care, does she? All she's interested in is that rotten old Dandini. What's he got that I haven't? (*To the audience*) I'm better than that swanky old tailor's dummy, aren't I, kids? Yes, of course I am. (*Sulkily*) Now she's got him, she doesn't want to know about *me* any more. She wouldn't even care if I went away and never came back again.

The Fairy Godmother enters in her normal costume

Fairy Godmother You're wrong, Buttons. Cinderella cares a great deal about you, but it is written that she must love another.

Buttons (*startled*) Blimey. It's ~~Mary Whitehouse.~~ *Barbara Cartland*

Fairy Godmother I am Cinderella's Fairy Godmother, and I come to ask a great favour of you.

Buttons Eh?

Fairy Godmother I want you to take special care of her, for very soon she will be needing your friendship more than anything else in the whole wide world.

Buttons You mean—even more than that Dandini fellow?

Fairy Godmother Much more, Buttons. Much, much more. Watch over her and give her all the help you can, for unless you do so, she will be more unhappy than she has ever been in her whole life.

Buttons Why? What's going to happen to her?

Fairy Godmother Her cruel stepmother and her two stepsisters will do everything in their power to drive her away from home and the ones she loves. Only *you* will be able to stop them.

Buttons Me? What about *you*? If you're a Fairy Godmother, why can't *you* stop them?

Fairy Godmother Because *I* cannot be there all the time to keep watch; but *you* can. I want you to be my assistant and take care of things whilst I am away. Will you do that for me, Buttons?

Buttons You mean—I'll be a sort of Deputy Sheriff?

Fairy Godmother (*smiling*) You could say that.

Buttons (*eagerly*) And can I have a badge? You know—a star to put on me jacket.

Fairy Godmother Of course. (*She hands him a silver star*)

Buttons (*pinning it on*) Cor, smashing.

Fairy Godmother Now remember—you must do your very best to protect her, but if things get too difficult for you, just call on me and I'll come to her aid.

Buttons How will I know where to find you?

Fairy Godmother Don't worry. I'll be anywhere you look for me.

The Fairy Godmother exits

Buttons Just a minute. Hey—Missis Fairy. Wait. I want to ask you something. (*He runs off after her*) Missis Fairy. Missis Fairy . . .

As Buttons exits, Ammer and Tongs enter at opposite sides of the glade. They are moving backwards with great stealth. As they reach C, they bump and both give loud screams of fear. They turn

Ammer (*relieved*) Tongs.

Tongs (*almost sobbing*) Ammer.

They look round cautiously

Ammer Have we lost 'em?

Tongs (*mopping his brow*) I think so. Phew, that was a close shave.

Ammer I thought we'd had it for the minute. Oh, I've never run so fast in my life.

Tongs Did you see the faces on them? If I had a face like that fat one, I'd hire somebody to steal it.

Ammer And if I'd a face like the other one, I'd hire myself out for Hallowe'en parties. I mean—it couldn't be the face she was born with. It must be a re-tread.

Tongs Well what are we going to do now? We can't go back to the Mansion with those two hanging about.

Ammer I've got it. We'll wait till that Ball begins at the Castle tonight, then we'll sneak into the Mansion and grab the lot.

Tongs Good idea.

Ammer All we have to do then is to sell it all, and we can go on that holiday we've been promising ourselves for the past five years. It'll be a piece of cake.

Tongs Oh, yes. Two weeks in Paris, and all those wonderful girls.

Ammer Two weeks in Paris? You've got to be joking. We're not going to Paris. We're going to Rome.

Tongs Rome? What's in Rome?

Ammer Ruins. Old magnificent ruins.

Asphyxia and Euthanasia enter

Asphyxia
Euthanasia } You called us? } (*Speaking together*)

Ammer
Tongs } Help. } (*Speaking together*)

Ammer and Tongs attempt to run, but are caught

Ammer Mercy.

Asphyxia It's no use trying to fight it. This thing is bigger than both of us.

Tongs What thing?

Euthanasia Her mouth. (*She purses her lips at Tongs*) Mmmmmmmmmm.

Asphyxia (*flinging Ammer aside and advancing on her sister*) Listen, foul-face. For the last time, I do *not* have a big mouth.

Euthanasia Darling—the only mouth *I* know that's bigger than yours, is the mouth of the Amazon River.

Asphyxia Is that so? (*She rolls up her sleeves*)

Euthanasia (*pushing Tongs aside*) Yes. Your mouth is so big you have to keep your false teeth in a *spare room*.

Asphyxia That is a *lie*. I keep them in a bucket at the side of the *bed*. And in any case—you've some need to talk. Your mouth is so big, you've had to have safety rails fitted to stop pot-holers from falling in.

Ammer and Tongs sidle off quietly

Euthanasia (*screeching*) Why, you grotty looking creep . . . (*She notices that the men are gone*) Oh—they've escaped.

Asphyxia (*spinning round*) Quick. After them.

Euthanasia Oh—let 'em go.

Asphyxia Are you crackers? They're MEN.

Euthanasia We can always get 'em tonight at the Ball.

Asphyxia (*shrugging*) Oh well—if that's the way you want it—you can have 'em both. I'll be too busy with the Prince to bother about *those* drips.

Euthanasia You? With the Prince? Don't make me laugh. Since when has he been interested in archaeology?

Asphyxia What do you mean, archaeology? I'm only just over the age of consent, and you know it.

Euthanasia You might be just over the age of consent, ducky, but from what I can see of you, you're heading for the age of collapse.

Asphyxia (*coldly*) For your information, frogspawn-features, there were only twenty-two candles on *my* last birthday cake.

Euthanasia And for *your* information, prune-face—there were twenty-two on my *slice*.

Asphyxia Oooh . . .!

Euthanasia Anyway—in case you'd forgotten—I do happen to be quite a *few* years younger than you.

Asphyxia And how do you work that out? Dividing by five?

Euthanasia (*sneering*) You can't upset me, darling. By the time tonight is over, I shall be the new Princess, and you'll be back where you belong. In the sewers.

Asphyxia Oh, yes? Well, we'll soon see about that, won't we? A few soft words breathed gently in the right direction, and the Prince will be lying at my feet.

Euthanasia I wouldn't be at all surprised. Your breath'll knock him unconscious. Anyway—I'm not staying here to argue with you. I'm off to prepare myself for the Ball. After all—my Prince awaits me.

Asphyxia In that case, I'd better pop down to the chemist's and buy him a little present, hadn't I?

Euthanasia (*suspiciously*) What sort of present?

Asphyxia Well—if he's going to meet *you* in full lighting, he's going to be in urgent need of what I'm going to get him.

Euthanasia What *is* it?

Asphyxia A case of smelling salts and a stomach pump.

Asphyxia exits. Euthanasia gives a fearful screech and charges after her, as—

the CURTAIN falls

SCENE 4

A Corridor in Stoneybroke Mansion   (Sawg 7)

The Dancers go through a Junior Miss routine in nightgowns and carrying candles

SCENE 5

The Kitchen of Stoneybroke Mansion

There is a large brick fireplace: the fire is low, and a kettle stands on the hob. In the middle of the room is a scrubbed kitchen table and three wooden chairs. A tablecloth covers the top of the table. To one side is a clothes-horse with a towel on it

Cinders is kneeling in the middle of the room, wearily washing the floor

Asphyxia (*off*) Cinderellaaaa!
Euthanasia (*off, on the opposite side*) Cinderellaaaaa!
Cinders (*standing and wiping her hands on her apron*) Coming.

Asphyxia enters

Asphyxia Oh, there you are, you lazy little creep. Fix my hair and look sharp about it.

Euthanasia enters

Euthanasia Never mind her tarred string. Get me my new ball gown.
Asphyxia (*loudly*) Hair!
Euthanasia (*louder*) Ball gown!
Asphyxia (*yelling*) Hair!
Euthanasia (*screeching*) Ball gown!
Cinders (*covering her ears*) Yes, yes, yes. (*She runs first one way then the other in confusion*)
Asphyxia (*grabbing her*) What's the matter with you?
Cinders I don't know which to do first.
Euthanasia Fetch my gown.
Asphyxia Do my hair. (*She twists Cinders' arm*)
Cinders Oh—you're hurting me.
Asphyxia I *will* hurt you in a minute, you idle good for nothing little halfwit. Now do as you're told. (*With great drama*) Oh, the *servants* these days.
Cinders (*pulling free*) I'm *not* your servant. And if you don't stop shouting at me, I won't help *either* of you.
Euthanasia (*wide-eyed*) Ooooh! We've got a *cheeky* one here, have we? Well, we all know how to deal with *her* sort, don't we, sister dear? (*She pushes Cinders flying into Asphyxia*)
Cinders (*knocked breathless*) Oh.
Asphyxia We certainly do. (*She grabs Cinders*) Did you see the way she just *attacked* me? She'll have to be taught a lesson, won't she? (*She hurls Cinders back at Euthanasia*)
Euthanasia (*catching her*) Trying to *kick* me, eh? (*She flings her back at her sister*)
Asphyxia And now she's trying to *claw* me.

She throws Cinders to the floor between them

Euthanasia That'll teach her to respect her betters.

Asphyxia (*to Cinders*) Now fetch my hairbrush and make it snappy. I've got to make myself beautiful for the Prince.

Cinders gets up, sobbing

Euthanasia Stop that snivelling. I don't want salt water all over my new gown. Go get it at once, while I put a new face on.

Asphyxia (*preening*) Thank goodness for that. I thought you were going to wear that dreadful old one for the rest of your life.

Euthanasia You can sneer—but at least *I've* still got a perfect complexion. Yours looks like the inside of an Aero bar.

Asphyxia Is that so? Well how come then that everyone tells me I look like an angel fallen down from the skies?

Euthanasia I've no idea—but if you're an angel fallen down from the skies, you must have landed on your face. I've seen less wrinkles in a dried up prune.

Asphyxia (*stung*) There isn't a wrinkle on my face.

Euthanasia Well—none that are visible, I admit.

Asphyxia (*pleased*) You see? (*She turns away*)

Euthanasia You've had your face lifted so many times, every time you sit down you leave ripples on the *sofa*.

Asphyxia (*spinning round*) Who said that?

Euthanasia (*pointing at Cinders*) She did.

Cinders No.

Euthanasia I heard her say it with these very lips.

Asphyxia Right. I'll show her. (*She advances on Cinders*) Come here.

Cinders (*backing away*) Oh, please. I didn't say *anything*.

Euthanasia (*eagerly*) Yes she did. (*To the audience*) Didn't she? (*Reaction*) Yes she did. She did. (*To Asphyxia*) Don't listen to 'em. They're lying. (*To the audience*) Creeps! Finks!

Asphyxia (*to the audience*) Did *she* say it? (*She indicates her sister*) This one? (*She glares at Euthanasia*)

Euthanasia Keep away from me, you glass-eyed toad. (*She backs away*)

Asphyxia (*advancing*) I'll beat you to death with your own false eyelashes.

Euthanasia (*screeching*) Mummy! Mummy!

Baroness Hardupp hurries in

Baroness What is it? What's the matter?

Euthanasia (*pointing at Cinders*) It's that little bothercauser. She's been calling my sweet little sister bad names, and I'm getting the blame from that rotten lot out there. (*She points into the audience*)

Baroness (*looking into the audience with a sneer*) What else can you expect from Council House tenants? (*She glares at Cinders*) So . . . She's started already, has she? I knew she was a troublemaker the moment I first set eyes on her. Well *I'll* fix her. (*To Cinders*) Get upstairs and change all the bedding. Then you can scrub the floors till they shine, wash all the dishes, bring in the coal, iron the curtains, polish the woodwork, clean the brasses, dust the portraits, clean the windows, sweep the drive, clear out the gutters, pick up all the leaves on the lawn, weed the garden, bake the bread and tidy up this kitchen. And when you've done that—you can clean out the stables.

Cinders But—but I'm going to the Ball.

Baroness You? Going to the Ball? Why, you scruffy little ragamuffin, I'm not having you go to the Ball with us. You'll show us up in front of the Prince.

Cinders But I've got a ticket. Look. (*She produces the ticket*)

Baroness Let me *see* that. (*She takes it and rips it in half*) Oh—my hand slipped. I'm so sorry.

Cinders (*stunned*) My ticket. (*She stoops to gather up the pieces*) You've torn up my ticket. (*She begins to sob*)

Asphyxia (*hurt*) Oh, Mother. There was no need for that. Poor little thing. You've broken her heart.

Euthanasia (*gaping*) What's got into her?

Asphyxia (*sternly*) You ought to be ashamed of yourself. Stopping her from going to the Ball.

Baroness (*anxiously*) Asphyxia, my love. Do you feel all right?

Asphyxia (*snapping*) Of course I feel all right. It's just that I can't stand spiteful people. (*She poses*) Anyway—I'll tell you what. *I'm* thinking of letting her go to the Ball after all.

Baroness (*horror-stricken*) You couldn't. You just *couldn't*.

Asphyxia I could. (*To the audience*) Shall I let Cinderella go to the Ball, kids? Shall I? (*Reaction*) And shall I lend her one of my beautiful frocks, as well? Shall I? (*To Cinders*) And would you like to go to the Ball with me, Cinderella dear, and leave old slug features there—(*she indicates Euthanasia*)—at home to see how *she* likes it?

Cinders (*dazed*) Oh yes, Asphyxia. I would. I would.

Asphyxia (*helping her up*) I thought so. You want to go to that Ball more than anything else in the world, don't you?

Cinders Oh, yes.

Asphyxia (*snapping*) Well that's just why you're *not going*, you foul-faced little creep. (*She screams with laughter*)

Cinders looks stunned and the others smirk

Baroness Come along now, girls. Let's go get ready.

The Baroness, Asphyxia and Euthanasia exit, laughing nastily

Cinders sinks to the floor sobbing, amongst the fragments of her ticket

The Baron enters

Baron (*seeing her*) Cinders. (*He hurries to her*) Don't cry, my love. What's wrong?

Cinders (*clinging to him*) Oh, Daddy. I wanted to go to the Ball tonight, but they won't let me.

Baron (*indignantly*) Of course you can go. It's nothing to do with them.

Off you go and get changed into a pretty dress. I'll take you to the Ball myself.

Cinders (*delighted*) Oh, Daddy. (*She kisses him and hurries off*)

Cinders hurries off

Baron (*rising*) I'll show them who's boss around here.

The Baroness enters

Baroness Oh? And who *is* the boss? (*She glares at him*)

Baron Oh—er—I—I . . . *You* are, my precious.

Baroness What were you saying to Cinderella just then?

Baron I—er—I was telling her that—that—(*defiantly*)—that she *could* come with us to the Ball.

Baroness Oh, you were, were you? And what makes you think that you're in any position to say who goes to the Ball and who doesn't?

Baron Because *I've* got the tickets, that's why. (*He waves four tickets*) They just came through the door.

Baroness Hand them over. (*She holds out her hand*)

Baron Is Cinderella going with us or not?

Baroness Of course she isn't.

Baron Right. (*He rips one of the tickets in pieces*) That leaves three.

Baroness (*horrified*) But there are *four* of us.

Baron There *were*. Now does Cinders go with us, or do I tear up another?

Baroness (*fuming*) Oh, all right. Now give me the tickets.

He hands over two tickets

But there's only two here. I need another one.

Baron Oh, no. This is for me. (*He waves the third ticket*) You can fight it out between you who gets the two *you've* got.

Baroness (*tartly*) And what about your precious Cinderella? Where is *her* ticket coming from? (*She smirks*) I've just torn it up.

Baron In that case, I'll have one of those tickets back, and your two can stay at home.

Baroness (*fiercely*) Never. If they can't have it, then nobody will. (*She swiftly tears the ticket up*) There.

Baron Now we've only two left.

Baroness One for me and one for you.

Baron Oh, no. One for me and one for Cinderella. Hand it over.

Baroness I'll die first. (*She rips up the other ticket*)

Baron You silly old faggot. Now there's only one left.

Baroness (*realizing*) It's all your fault. You drove me to it.

Baron There's only one thing I'd like to drive you to, and that's the edge of a cliff. Oh, how I wish I'd never married you.

Baroness (*wailing*) Owwww!

The Baroness exits in tears

Baron One ticket. (*He looks at it*) Now what are we going to do?

The Baron exits, puzzled. Buttons enters from the other side

Buttons (*calling*) Yoo-hoo. Anybody home?

The Sisters enter, in their underwear

Asphyxia What are you screaming at, pipsqueak?
Buttons There's a man, without.
Euthanasia Without what?
Buttons He says he wants an audience.
Asphyxia Well give him *this* dozy lot. (*She indicates the audience*)
Buttons (*patiently*) Well, do I ask him in or don't I? He's from the Castle.
Both Sisters From the Castle? Oh, it's the Prince for me. (*They fuss*)
Buttons (*shaking his head*) I'd better show him in.

Buttons exits

Euthanasia Quick. I must put something on.
Asphyxia Try a mask.
Euthanasia You've some need to talk. You should have been born in the Dark Ages. You look terrible in the light.

Dandini enters

Dandini Good evening. (*He realizes*) Good night. (*He turns to flee*)
Both Sisters (*screaming with delight*) The Prince!

They lurch into a curtsy, collide and crash to the floor

Dandini (*pausing and turning*) I—er—I was actually looking for the daughter of Baron Hardupp.
Both Sisters That's me.
Dandini I. mean—the *youngest* daughter.
Both Sisters That's me.
Dandini (*embarrassed*) Isn't there *another* daughter?
Both Sisters No. Just me.
Dandini Then I seem to have been misled.
Asphyxia (*delighted*) Oh, you saucy old thing you. (*She pushes him playfully and knocks him flying*)
Dandini (*recovering himself*) I—er—I'd better be going. The—er—the Ball, you know.
Euthanasia I shall look forward to dancing every dance with you, your Principality. (*She simpers*)
Asphyxia Yes—she'll be very light on your feet—providing you dance on your hands. Dance with me instead.
Dandini I'm sorry, ladies. I'm afraid I shall be in very great demand. I'm very well known, you understand. All the ladies love me, and to tell you the truth, I love them all in return.

SONG 9

After the song, Dandini exits. Cinders enters in a rather pretty, but very worn dress

Cinders I'm ready. (*She displays the dress*)

Asphyxia (*turning to her*) And where do you think *you're* going to, little miss droopy-drawers?

Cinders I—I'm going to the Ball with you. Daddy said he'd take me. (*Eagerly*) Do you like the dress? Will it be all right?

Euthanasia Dress? DRESS? I've seen better looking *floorcloths*. (*She grabs hold of a sleeve and rips it out*) Oh . . . (*She smiles in mock sorrow*) I *am* sorry.

Cinders (*clutching at her arm in shock*) My dress.

Asphyxia Never mind, dear. I'll soon make it match. (*She rips out the other sleeve*)

Cinders (*trying to escape*) No, no. Stop it.

Euthanasia (*grabbing her*) That's a fine way to thank us for helping her, isn't it?

Asphyxia The absolute ingratitude of the child. Besides—look at that belt. Belts are out. (*She rips off Cinders' belt*)

Euthanasia So are BACKS. (*She rips out the back of the dress*)

Cinders (*pulling free in tears*) No, no, no. (*She exits, crying*)

Asphyxia (*tittering*) That's fixed her. Come along, sister dear. Let's get ready.

Euthanasia Our public is waiting.

Linking arms with huge smirks, Asphyxia and Euthanasia exit. Buttons enters and glares after them

Buttons Poor old Cinders. I'll make 'em sorry for what they've just done. (*To the audience*) Fancy spoiling her party dress to stop her going to the Ball. Still—I'll have her all to meself while they're away, won't I? We can have a little party all on our own. Just us and the kiddies. I've got a little bag of crisps, and a bruised apple—and there's bound to be a bit of cheese left in one of the mouse-traps. Oh, we'll have a smashing time, won't we, kids? Lots better than that mouldy old party at the Castle.

Cinders enters, wiping her eyes

Cinders I hate them. I *hate* them.

Buttons (*going to her*) Don't cry, Cinders. There'll be another Ball one day, and I'll take you there myself, honest I will.

Cinders But it's *this* Ball I want to go to, Buttons. Dandini will be waiting for me.

Buttons Dandini. (*Disgusted*) Well in that case, I hope he waits forever.

Cinderella begins to cry again

Oh, I'm sorry. I didn't mean it. Don't cry, Cinders. Please.

Cinders (*moving to the fire*) I'm so unhappy. (*She sinks to the floor in front of the flames*)

Buttons Well, it's no use sitting there crying about it. That won't help matters. Honestly—I've never known such a small girl have so many tears in her. Now come on. Cheer up.

SONG 10

Take it on the chin
(Me & my girl)

Cinders (*smiling*) I feel a lot better now, thanks to you.
Buttons Good. Now let's see you keep that smile.

The Baron, Baroness, Asphyxia and Euthanasia enter in their finery

Baroness (*loudly*) Well, we're off.
Buttons I thought something smelled around here.
Baroness (*ignoring him*) See this place is tidied up by the time we get back.
Baron (*comforting Cinders*) Good night, my pet. I'll try to bring you a little slice of cake back.
Asphyxia Oh, come on. My Prince is waiting for me.
Euthanasia Listen to Snow White. (*She follows her sister doorwards*) Just you pin your great lugholes back and listen to me, you two-faced cat . . .

Asphyxia and Euthanasia exit, arguing loudly

Baroness Come along, Percival. And don't forget to wash your hands now that you've touched her.

The Baroness sweeps out

Baron (*kissing Cinders*) Bye-bye, love. (*To Buttons*) Look after her, Buttons.

The Baron exits brokenly

Buttons (*after a pause*) Well—they've gone. Off to the Ball.
Cinders (*softly*) Yes.

There is a short silence as the room darkens

Buttons Cinders?

No reply

Sure you're all right?

No reply

Shall I put some more wood on the fire for you? I think it's going out

No reply

Oh come on, Cinders. Say something to me.
Cinders (*shivering*) Oh, Buttons. It's so gloomy and cold in here.
Buttons (*eagerly*) Here. Take my coat. (*He takes off his coat to reveal a very patched shirt beneath it*) Put this round your shoulders. (*He drapes it round her*) There—isn't that better?
Cinders Yes, thank you.
Buttons (*shyly*) I say—Cinders. Shall *we* have a party? Just the two of us? All by ourselves?
Cinders (*uninterested*) If you like.
Buttons (*peeved*) Enthusiastic, aren't you?
Cinder (*trying to make amends*) Oh, I'm sorry, Buttons. It's just that I wanted to ride in a coach like a great lady for once.
Buttons Oh, is that all? Well, we can soon fix that. (*He gets one of the chairs*) Now this is a coach. You sit here. Come on.

She sits without much interest

Now then—we want some horses, don't we? (*He gets the clothes-horse and places it in front of her*) There. (*He gets another chair and places it beside her*) And I'll be the coachman. (*He slips his arm around her*) NOW- giddy-up.

They both laugh, but after a moment Cinders sighs

Cinders But it's not the same, is it?
Buttons Ah, we haven't finished yet. Come on. Get out of the coach. (*He assists her out*) Now then,—I'll be Prince Charming—(*he bows*)—and you'll be Princess Cinderella.

Cinders curtsies

Oh—hang on a minute—we've forgotten your Ball gown. (*He hurries to the table, gets the cloth and ties it round her waist*) And now—will you dance with me, Princess Cinderella?
Cinders (*regally*) Which dance shall we do, Your Highness?
Buttons Well it'd better be the one you taught me this afternoon, 'cos I don't know any others. This way to the dance hall.

He leads her forward, and they dance together for a few moments enjoying it. Suddenly Cinders bursts into tears again and tears free. She runs to the fireplace

Cinders?
Cinders (*sobbing*) Go away.
Buttons But Cinders . . .
Cinders (*louder*) Go away.
Buttons (*peeved*) All right, then. I will. And I'll have me coat back, as well. (*He takes it*) Tara, then. (*Pause*) Cinders? I'm going. (*Pause*) Cinders?

Cinders continues to sob quietly

Sadly and slowly, Buttons exits

Cinders sinks to the floor and the room grows darker still

The Village Children enter slowly, wearing their night things

Girl What's the matter, Cinderella? Why are you crying?
Cinders (*quickly drying her tears*) What are you doing downstairs? You should all be in bed.
Boy We came to say good night to you.

SONG 11

This could be "Good night, Cinders", sung to the tune of "Good night, Sweetheart"

At the end of the song the Children all kiss Cinders and exit. Buttons enters in a great rush

Buttons (*excitedly*) I've got it. I've got it. Don't go away.

Buttons dashes out through the main door

Cinders (*standing*) Buttons—Buttons . . . (*Bewildered*) Whatever is he talking about?

There are three loud knocks on the main door

Who's there?

The Old Lady of the woods enters

Old Lady It is I, my child. The old lady of the woods.

Cinders (*hurrying to her*) But you shouldn't be out on a cold night like this. Please—sit by the fireside, and I'll try to find you a bowl of warm soup, or something.

Old Lady Wait. *You* gave me *your* aid in the woods, and now *I* come to keep *my* promise to *you*. Tell me—what is your heart's desire? Name it, and it shall be yours.

Cinders My heart's desire? Oh, to go to the Ball tonight. But how can you help me to do that?

Old Lady Simple. (*She throws off her cloak*) I am your Fairy Godmother.

Cinders steps back in surprise

Fear not, my child. Your good friend Buttons called on me and told me of your plight. Because you are kind hearted and honest, you *shall* go to the Ball. Your wish will be *granted*.

Cinders (*bewildered*) But—how?

Fairy Godmother Just do as I say, and all will be well. First go to the cellar and bring me a large pumpkin, six white mice and two lizards.

Cinders hurries off

With the aid of a little magic, these things will be changed into the most wonderful coach and horses that the world has ever seen. Not to mention the two most handsome footmen.

Cinders enters with the things

Cinders Here they are.

Fairy Godmother Place them in the fireplace, my child.

Cinders does so

And now to arrange for your ball gown. (*She waves her wand*)

A host of Fairies enter from all sides

Take this child and make her the finest gown that mortal eyes have ever seen.

Two Fairies lead Cinders out

Weave the thread from thistledown, and give her a mantle of Stardust. Take Moonbeams for her Coronet, and dress her hair with the stars themselves.

There follows the Ballet of the Fairies

As it finishes, Cinders enters in her finery, but still wearing her old shoes

Ah, charming, my dear. Absolutely charming. But one more thing. (*She waves her wand*)

A Fairy enters with a pair of crystal slippers

Take this pair of crystal slippers, for they are made of fairy music, and will allow you to dance any dance you will. (*She turns*) And now for the coach. (*She waves her wand again*)

The Lights go out. There is a flash. The Lights go up again to reveal a golden coach drawn by six Children dressed as horses, with two liveried Footmen emerging from the fireplace. The other things have gone. A Footman opens the door to the coach

Off you go, my child. Enjoy yourself. But remember this warning. The spell will end at midnight, so you must leave in time to get back here. Should you forget, your fine clothes will turn back to rags and your coach, horses and footmen will vanish into thin air. Do you understand?
Cinders (*breathlessly*) Oh, yes. And thank you. Thank you a million times. (*She gets into the coach*)
Fairy Godmother Remember. Twelve o'clock. (*She waves her wand and the coach moves off*)

Cinders waves out of the coach window as the Fairies form a tableau. The Fairy Godmother showers stardust as—

the CURTAIN *falls*

ACT II

SCENE 1

SONG 9

The CURTAIN rises on a cloth of the outside of the Castle. Crowds of people are arriving at the gates, in procession to appropriate music. Footmen are standing at each side of the gates taking tickets as they are produced. The Guests then pass into the Castle grounds. The last ones enter, leaving only the two Footmen on duty. The Baron and Baroness enter in a hurry

Baroness Hurry up, or the Ball will be over before we get there.

Baron Well that's one way of making sure it'll be a successful party.

Baroness Where are my little angels? (*She looks round impatiently*)

Baron (*aside*) I know where I'd *like* them to be.

Asphyxia and Euthanasia enter: one carries Ammer, the other carries Tongs

Asphyxia (*delighted*) Look what *we* found in the garden!

Euthanasia (*ecstatic*) MEN!

They put the men down, but cling on to them tightly

Baroness It's those horrible Broker's Men. Why did you bring *them*?

Baron Obvious. The poor fools couldn't *run* fast enough.

Asphyxia (*ignoring this*) What do you mean—"Why did we bring them"? They're *breathing*, aren't they? And besides—you don't think we're going to come to a Ball without *escorts*, do you?

Euthanasia We might get pounced on in the dark, and carried off. With a bit of luck. (*She giggles*)

Ammer Well you needn't worry about that. If anybody pounced on you two in the dark and carried you off, they'd drop you like a shot as soon as they got you under a lamp-post.

Baroness (*stung*) Really. I don't know how you can stand there and insult my precious little darlings like that.

Tongs It's easy. He just opens his mouth.

Euthanasia Oh, shut up and let's get inside.

Baroness Euthanasia is right. The Prince will be expecting us.

Baron Yes. He'll be having the doorway bricked up.

Asphyxia Well—where are the tickets?

Euthanasia Mother's got them, haven't you, dear? (*She holds out her hand*)

Baroness Well—er—there seems to have been a slight *mistake*.

Sisters Mistake?

Baroness (*smiling weakly*) There's only *one* ticket.

Baron (*holding it up*) *This* one.

The Sisters look aghast

Baroness I—er—I had a little *accident* with the rest.

Euthanasia Oh, what a pity. Never mind though. I'll tell you what it was like when I get home again. (*She snatches the ticket*)

Asphyxia (*snatching the ticket from her*) Not so fast, bandylegs. If anybody's going in there, it's *me*. The Prince is expecting a vision of loveliness. (*She simpers*)

Tongs In that case, you'd better let *me* go in.

Asphyxia (*rounding on him*) And what's that supposed to mean? Let me tell you, I could have been the biggest thing in Hollywood Screen History with my looks.

Euthanasia Yes, but they found *King Kong* first.

Baron Oh, give over, you two. We'll never get in at *this* rate.

Ammer And I'm freezing. I must be standing in a draught.

Baron You are. (*To the Baroness*) Close your mouth, Medusa.

Baroness I was just about to say that we'll have to think up some way to outwit these footmen. (*She thinks*) I've got it. Quickly, now. All look upwards as though you've seen something.

Tongs What sort of something?

Baroness Anything. Anything at all. (*Loudly*) Oh—look . . .

Everyone looks up, including the two Footmen

The Baroness suddenly slips past them and exits into the Castle

Euthanasia (*looking down again*) *I* can't see a thing. (*She sees her mother is missing*) Oh—she's gone.

Everyone looks down, and the Footmen spring back into position

Asphyxia Well, the crafty old cat. She must have slipped inside.

Baron Quick. Let's try again.

All look up as before

The Baron slips into the Castle grounds

Euthanasia (*grumbling*) I still don't know what we're supposed to be looking at. And I'm getting a stiff . . . (*She looks down*) Oh—now *he's* gone.

All look down again and the Footmen revert to their positions

Asphyxia (*excitedly*) Right. Same routine, everybody, and I'll get in.

Ammer Not likely.

Tongs You see—*we've* got tickets. (*He produces two tickets*)

Ammer and Tongs hand the tickets to the Footmen and pass through

Euthanasia The rotten cheats. Now there's only *us* left outside.

Asphyxia You mean there's only *you*, don't you, ducky? *I've* got a ticket, too. (*She displays it*)

Euthanasia You don't mean to say you're going inside and leaving me stuck out here, do you?

Asphyxia I certainly *do*. (*She sails regally towards the Footmen*)
Euthanasia Wait. Let's do the routine just one more time, and I promise I'll tell the audience the truth about my age.
Asphyxia (*pausing*) You *will*?
Euthanasia (*nodding tearfully*) Promise.
Asphyxia (*triumphantly*) O.K. (*She indicates the audience*) Go ahead. I'm listening.
Euthanasia (*softly*) I'm twenty-three . . .

Asphyxia moves towards the Footmen

Twenty-six.

Asphyxia keeps moving

Thirty-seven.

Asphyxia holds out her ticket

FIFTY-EIGHT.

Asphyxia returns with a big smile

Asphyxia There. Now, that wasn't too bad, was it? *Fifty-eight*. (*To the audience*) She can remember Heinz when he had only *four* varieties— (*to Euthanasia*)—can't you, dear?
Euthanasia All right. All right. There's no need to rub it in. Let's get on with the routine. Now what do we do?
Asphyxia We look up into the air, stupid.
Euthanasia Like this? (*She looks out into the audience*)
Asphyxia No, no. It'll never work if you look like that. You look up like this. (*She looks upwards, holding the ticket loosely*) Get yourself an eyeful. (*Suddenly she claps her empty hand to her eye*) Owwww! You dirty rotten seagull.
Euthanasia (*snatching the ticket*) That's the only eyeful *you're* going to get tonight, darling.

Euthanasia dashes off, tossing the ticket to the Footmen

Asphyxia (*screeching*) Come back.

Asphyxia charges after her, pushing aside the Footmen, who recover and give chase. As they exit, Cinders enters, followed by Buttons

Cinders Thank you for coming with me, Buttons. I'll never forget what you've done for me. Never.
Buttons Not even when you're dancing with that rotten old Dandini?
Cinders (*happily*) Not even then. (*She kisses him on the cheek*)
Buttons (*almost swooning*) Ohhhhh! (*Recovering*) I'd better be getting back to the children, now, hadn't I? I can't keep all those fairies hanging about, even if they *did* promise to do all the work for us. (*He moves away*) And Cinders . . .
Cinders Yes?
Buttons You look smashing. Honest.

Cinders Thank you. (*She moves towards the gates*)

Buttons moves a little further away, then turns suddenly

Buttons Oh, and Cinders . . .
Cinders (*turning to him*) Yes?
Buttons Will you do something for me?
Cinders Of course I will. What is it?
Buttons Well—it's something silly. (*He squirms with embarrassment*)
Cinders I don't mind.
Buttons Honest?
Cinders Honest.
Buttons Well—will you bring me some jam tarts back from the party?
Cinders (*laughing*) As many as you like.
Buttons Thanks. (*He edges away again*) Well—tara, then.
Cinders Tara. (*She turns to go again*)
Buttons (*suddenly*) Cinders . . .
Cinders (*turning again*) Yes?
Buttons You nearly forgot your ticket. (*He pulls it out of his pocket*)
Cinders (*realizing*) Oh, thank you. (*She takes it gently*)
Buttons (*gazing at her lovingly*) Have a nice time, Cinders.

Cinders smiles and nods, then turns and exits into the Castle grounds

Buttons stands looking after her

(*Softly*) Take care. (*He turns dejectedly away from the gates*) Rotten old
Dandini.

SONG 12 (*a sad ballad*)

At the end of the song the Lights fade

Buttons exits, on the verge of tears

SCENE 2

The Ballroom of Castle Glamorous

*The room is filled with Guests, laughing, talking and drinking champagne.
Footmen drift around with trays of champagne glasses. The Major Domo is
at the top of a short flight of stairs leading down to the ballroom, and behind
him can be seen a large clock with the hands at nine-fifteen. Music is playing*

SONG 13 (*optional, for Dandini and the Chorus*)

As the song ends, the Major Domo announces new arrivals

Major Domo Lady Bird and Count Twenty-four.

The Guests enter

Sir Watt Fitz-Hugh Fitz-Herbert—and Herbert.

The Guests enter. The Prince enters and moves to Dandini

Prince Dandini—has she arrived yet?

Dandini I'm afraid not, Your Highness.

Prince What can be keeping her? Oh, Dandini—if she doesn't arrive soon, I know I'm just going to *burst*. Now I wish you could have seen her. She's the most beautiful girl in the world.

Dandini And you're quite sure she told you she was the Baron Hardupp's daughter, Sire? I mean—the ones *I* saw were like the left-overs from last week's dinner.

Prince (*laughing*) Dandini! (*Briskly*) Now keep a sharp look out for her and let me know the moment she arrives. I must pay a little attention to some of our other guests. (*He moves away*)

Dandini (*musing*) Mmmmm. He has got it badly. (*He moves to chat with guests again*)

Major Domo (*announcing*) Baron and Baroness Hardupp and their daughters,

The Prince and Dandini spin round

Asphyxia and Euthanasia.

The Prince and Dandini exchange looks

And—

The Prince and Dandini look up again

Mr Ammer and Mr Tongs.

The Baron and Baroness, Asphyxia, Euthanasia, Ammer and Tongs enter

Prince (*to Dandini*) I don't understand. Where is she?

Asphyxia (*crying out from the stairs*) Yoo-hoo, Prinny. I'm here.

Euthanasia (*pushing her aside*) Out of the way, repulsive. (*She runs downstairs and grabs Dandini in a fierce embrace*) Come on, Prinny. Lets swing it. (*She lurches into a dance with the struggling Dandini*)

Dandini (*pushing her off*) Let go of me, woman. I'm afraid you've made a mistake. I am Dandini, the Prince's valet. This—(*he indicates the Prince*) —is His Highness.

Euthanasia (*taken aback*) What? Old sparrowlegs? But you said in the woods—you—er—he . . . (*She realizes*) Oh, no.

Asphyxia (*sweeping down in triumph*) *I* knew it all the time. Come on, handsome. Let's sit down and discuss our wedding plans. (*She links arms with him*)

Prince (*angrily*) Unhand me at once, woman. How dare you lay hands on me?

Asphyxia quickly lets go of him

Baroness (*hurrying forwards*) Oh, please forgive them, Your Washupp. It's their father's bad manners coming out.

Prince (*coldly*) Very well. But see that it does not occur again.

The Sisters pull faces at him behind his back, but adopt innocent smiles when he turns round again

Come, Dandini. We'll go into the other room.

The Prince and Dandini exit

Asphyxia (*mocking savagely*) "Come, Dandini. We'll go into the other room". (*She sneers*) Who does he think he is? (*Well-known "pop" singer*)
Baroness It's no use getting upset, darling. You'll realize one day that some people have *no* manners at all.
Euthanasia (*sniffing*) You can say *that* again.
Baroness Now what we've got to do, is to think of a way to get him to propose to one of you. Let's go into the garden and work on a plan.

The Baroness and Sisters exit

Baron (*moving down with the Broker's Men*) I wonder what they're up to?
Ammer I don't know—but I bet it's something horrible.
Baron Why have they gone into the garden?
Tongs To frighten the bats away?
Baron If you ask me, there's something brewing out there.
Ammer By the looks of those three, it'll probably be a cauldron.
Major Domo (*announcing*) The Princess Crystal.

Cinders enters

Everyone gasps

Ammer⎱
Tongs⎰ Cor . . . ⎱(*Speaking together*)

The Prince enters

Baron (*gaping at Cinders*) It can't be. It's impossible.
Prince (*hurrying forwards*) Princess. (*He bows to her*) Welcome to the Castle. I am Prince Charming.
Cinders (*in the middle of her curtsy*) Prince Charming? But I thought . . . (*She recovers herself*) Your Highness. (*She completes her curtsy*)
Prince Allow me to take your arm.
Cinders Why, thank you.

The Prince leads her on to the main floor

Prince I'm so glad you came, Your Highness. The evening looked dull before you appeared, but now *your* presence makes the whole Castle look brighter.
Cinders Thank you, Your Highness, but I fear I may be intruding. You see—I was not invited as the Princess Crystal.
Prince What is an invitation to someone as beautiful as you? You are welcome to remain here for as long as you wish. And now may I ask you to dance?
Cinders You may—and I accept.

Everyone swirls into a waltz. The Lights lower to indicate time passing, then come up again. It is now eleven o'clock. The Baron is downstage, dazed

(*Laughing*) Oh, I'm absolutely exhausted. Do you mind if we rest for a while?

Prince As you wish, Princess. We will adjourn to the Conservatory whilst the members of the Royal Ballet entertain our guests.

The Prince and Cinders exit

The Royal Ballet entertain

After the entertainment, the Royal Ballet exit

Major Domo (*announcing*) Dinner will be served shortly in the Golden Hall. Would you kindly take your places.

All exit but the Baron

Baron (*shaking his head*) I could have sworn that the Princess was my little Cinderella—but how could it have been? (*Sighing*) Oh, how I wish she'd been able to come tonight.

The Baron exits slowly after the others. As he does so, Cinders and the Prince enter

Prince And to think that only this morning I thought I had fallen in love.
Cinders In love? With whom?
Prince A young girl I met in the woods during the hunt. She didn't realize that I was the Prince. In fact, I led her to believe that I was Dandini, my own valet.
Cinders Wasn't that wrong of you?
Prince I suppose it was, but it made such a change to be liked for myself, and not because I happen to be a Prince.
Cinders And will you be seeing this girl again?
Prince Oh, no. Not now that I've found *you*.
Cinders (*mocking gently*) I see. Prince Charming has a fickle heart.
Prince Not any more, I promise you.

Dandini enters briskly

Dandini Your Highness . . . (*He sees Cinderella*) Oh—I *do* beg your pardon.
Prince (*smiling*) Dandini. Allow me to introduce you to the Princess Crystal—and, I hope—my future bride.
Dandini (*bowing low*) Your Highness.
Prince You wanted me for something?
Dandini Yes, Your Highness. I came to tell you that the guests were assembled and the feast is about to begin.
Prince Then we'd better come at once. Princess? (*He takes her arm*)

The Prince and Cinders exit

Dandini (*as he exits*) He's soon changed his tune. From village girl to a Princess in one day. Ah, well—prerogative of a Prince, I suppose.

Dandini exits after the Prince. The Baroness and the Sisters enter

Baroness Now remember what I've told you . . . (*She looks round in surprise*) Oh—they've all gone.

Asphyxia (*annoyed*) I knew it. The minute we turn our backs they dash off and start shovelling the food down their gullets. (*To the Baroness*) Thanks to you and your "Lets go into the garden", we probably won't even get a bite to eat.

Euthanasia And I'm starving. Not to mention freezing cold. I'm probably going to catch a nasty cold.

Asphyxia You may as well while you've got the chance. You'll never manage to catch the Prince, and *that's* for sure.

Euthanasia You've some need to talk, you foul faced freak. If I were a feller and you were the last woman on earth, I wouldn't even give you a second look.

Asphyxia If I were a feller and *you* were the last woman on earth, I'd certainly give *you* one. I'd want to make sure I wasn't seeing things.

Baroness Girls, girls. Really. You mustn't fight like this. Remember—one of you is going to be the new Princess. The First Lady of the land.

Euthanasia (*sighing happily*) You do mean *me* of course, don't you?

Asphyxia Of course she does.

Euthanasia (*startled*) Eh?

Asphyxia I said *of course* she thinks you ought to be First Lady of the land. So do I.

Euthanasia You *do*?

Asphyxia Well, why not? After all—you are the *oldest* one.

Euthanasia (*enraged*) Why you . . .

Baroness (*sharply*) Euthanasia. Hold your tongue.

Asphyxia But mind you don't *bite* it, or you'll die of blood poisoning.

Baroness Quiet.

The Sisters glare at each other

Now then. Don't you think it would be a good idea to practice what you're going to do for the Prince?

Asphyxia (*peeved*) Oh, all right. But if I don't get a proposal before tonight's out, *somebody's* going to suffer.

Euthanasia You'll get a proposal, all right. They'll propose you go somewhere else to do your torturing.

Baroness Torturing? But she's going to sing.

Euthanasia Exactly.

Asphyxia And I suppose you'll be doing your *inimitable* rendering of the *Dying Duck* again?

Euthanasia And why not?

Asphyxia Well one look at you performing, and they'll know what it's dying of—dropsy.

Baroness Girls. (*Sweetly*) Now listen. I've just had a marvellous idea.

The Sisters gaze upwards with long-suffering looks

Asphyxia, darling—wouldn't you like to do something with your sister?

Asphyxia Don't *tempt* me.

Baroness I mean—why not do a *double* act?

Asphyxia }(*aghast*) *What?* }(*Speaking together*)
Euthanasia

Baroness A combined effort. (*Pressing*) I don't suppose the Prince has ever seen a combined effort before.

Euthanasia I don't know about a combined effort. *She* looks more like a combined harvester.

Baroness (*desperately*) You could do a duet—or Sphyxi could sing while you play on the piano.

Asphyxia She couldn't even play on the *lino. I'll* sing on my own, if you *don't* mind.

Euthanasia Yes. The minute she opens her cakehole, she *will* be on her own. They'll all buzz off.

Asphyxia Listen who's talking. The one-note wonder herself. Couldn't carry a tune if it had handles on it.

Euthanasia That's a lie. I could have been an opera singer if I hadn't had to give up singing because of throat trouble.

Asphyxia *Throat trouble.* We all know what trouble that was, don't we, ducky? The neighbours threatened to *cut it* for you.

Baroness Please . . .

The Baron enters

Baron Ah, there you are. The dinner's over.

The Baroness and Sisters begin to argue

The Guests and the Royals enter

Dandini (*cheerfully*) And now let the festivities begin in earnest. Bring in the entertainers.

All applaud except Baroness and Sisters

Baroness (*quickly*) Wait . . .

Everyone looks at her

I have a lovely surprise for you all.

Prince A surprise? What is it?

Baroness Something that will make you all very, very happy.

Baron She's going home and taking those two with her.

Baroness (*glaring at him*) My two talented daughters will now entertain for you.

Dandini (*groaning*) Oh, no.

The Guests look at each other in dismay

Prince (*quickly*) I'm afraid the entertainment has all been laid on and we haven't much time . . .

Baroness Oh, it won't take a moment. (*To the Sisters*) Quickly, girls. Show the Prince your talents.

The Sisters entertain as required. While they do so the Lights are lowered and the clock hands are changed to 11.50. At the end of the "Entertainment" the Lights return to full, and reveal the Guests in various stages of boredom. They applaud listlessly

(*Beaming*) And now I think we'll just slip out and refresh ourselves before we do the *Encore*.

The Guests look aghast

The Baroness and Sisters exit

Prince Dandini—we must do something. Get rid of them.
Dandini Don't worry, Your Highness. Leave it to me.

Dandini exits

Baron (*peering at Cinders*) It *is* her, I *know* it is. (*He begins to move towards her*)
Prince (*calling*) Music, if you please.

Music begins and the Prince swirls Cinders off in a waltz. Other Guests join in. The Major Domo returns to the top of the stair-case

Dandini hurries back and goes to whisper to the Major Domo

The Major Domo bangs his stick. The music stops

Major Dome (*announcing*) Ladies and Gentlemen. I have just been informed that certain people have entered this Castle without invitation cards. The Footmen will be coming around in just a moment to identify them. Would you please remain where you are.
Guests (*shocked*) Oh! Disgraceful! Shocking, etc.
Baron (*to Ammer and Tongs*) We've got to get out of here. Quick. Call the others.

Ammer and Tongs dash off

The Footmen begin to search the crowd. The Prince, Dandini and Cinders chat

The Baroness hurries in, followed by the Sisters

Baroness What is it?
Baron We've been spotted. Run for it.
Asphyxia (*panic-stricken*) I can't.
Euthanasia Neither can I.
Baron You must, or we're done for.
Asphyxia Well don't blame *me*.

Asphyxia lurches forwards. A shower of knives and forks fall from inside her gown. Everyone looks at her and them

Euthanasia (*horrified*) Asphyxia! How *could* you? (*She moves and a shower of spoons fall to the floor*)
Baroness Run for it.

The Baron, Baroness and Sisters dash up the stairs and out

Dandini (*calling*) Stop them.
Prince (*laughing*) Too late. They've gone.

The Footmen begin gathering up the cutlery

Now the party can *really* start to come alive.

The waltz music begins again and everyone joins in the dance. Coloured lights swirl and the laughter is loud. The clock hands are moved to midnight and it begins to chime

(*Twirling Cinders down* C) Midnight striking, and the night is still young.
Cinders (*surprised*) Midnight? (*She glances at the clock*) Oh—I must go. (*She pulls away from the Prince*)
Prince (*laughing*) Go? Nonsense. (*He tries to restrain her*)
Cinders But I must. I must. (*She turns to run*)
Prince But Princess . . .
Cinders Let me go, *please*. (*She pulls free and hurries up the stairs*)
Prince (*calling*) How can I find you again?

The Guests stare in astonishment

Princess. Princess . . .

Cinders dashes off L, *and a double, dressed in her original ragged dress runs back on, hands over her face, and exits* R

Princess . . . (*He hurries up the staircase*)
Dandini (*following him*) Your Highness . . .

Dandini and the Prince exit

The music comes to a halt. The Guests converse excitedly

Dandini and the Prince return

Prince It's no use, Dandini. She seems to have vanished into thin air.
Dandini (*escorting him downstage*) Perhaps the guards saw her leave, Your Highness. We'll know in a moment.

A Footman from the gates comes hurrying in

Well?
Footman There's no sign of the Princess Crystal at all, Your Highness. The Guards saw no-one but a young girl in a ragged dress.
Prince But that's impossible. He must have seen the Princess.

A second Footman enters, carrying a glass slipper

Second Footman I found this on the stairs, Your Highness. (*He displays it*)
Prince Dandini—her slipper. (*He takes it*) It must have fallen off as she ran. (*He hands it to Dandini*) Take it. Search the entire land for the one whose foot it came from. (*To the Guests*) Ladies and Gentlemen. I swear before all of you that the person this glass slipper fits shall be my future bride.

The Guests react

Now hurry, Dandini. Find her and bring her back to my arms.

A Footman enters with a silk cushion

Dandini places the slipper on the cushion and, holding the cushion firmly, moves up the staircase. At the top he turns and displays it to the Guests

Dandini exits, followed by the Footman

The Guests all chatter excitedly, as—

the CURTAIN *falls*

SCENE 3

On the way home from the Ball

Cinders, in her ragged dress, runs across the stage and exits. The Baron, Baroness, Sisters, Ammer and Tongs enter

Baroness I've never been so ashamed in my whole life. Chased out of a Royal Ball.

Euthanasia Just as I'd made a hit with the Prince, too.

Asphyxia Why do you think *you're* kidding, prune-features? The Prince couldn't keep his eyes off *me* all night.

Euthanasia I'm not surprised. It's the first time he's seen anything like you outside a zoo.

Baron Oh, give over, you two. The only one the Prince looked at was that beautiful Princess Crystal.

Ammer Cor, yes. Wasn't she smashing?

Tongs Not half.

Asphyxia Some folks have strange ideas about beauty, don't they? *I* thought she looked like an accident looking for somewhere to happen.

Euthanasia She'd so many wrinkles, I bet she has to screw her hats on.

Ammer Well, we thought she looked smashing, didn't we Tongs?

Tongs Just like a dream.

Euthanasia More like a nightmare, if you ask me.

Baroness (*thoughtfully*) You know—there was something very strange about *her.*

Ammer (*looking at Euthanasia*) There still is.

Baroness Fool. I meant the other one.

Tongs (*looking at Asphyxia*) Yes—I see what you mean.

Baroness I'm sure I've seen her somewhere *before*, that Princess Crystal.

Baron (*nervously*) Don't be silly, Medusa. How could you have? After all—how many Princesses do you know?

Baroness She wasn't a Princess when *I* knew her—she was a—a . . . Oh, what *was* it? Let me think.

Asphyxia Well if you ask *me*—it looked like a cleaned up version of that little drip Cinderella.

Baron (*quickly*) Oh, no. That's impossible. Out of the question.

Baroness (*light dawning*) That's it. *Cinderella.*

Euthanasia Are you out of your tiny mind? How could it have been? We left her at home scrubbing out the kitchen, didn't we?

Baroness We *thought* we did. (*Her eyes narrowing*) Quickly . . . back to the Mansion.

Baron But Medusa, my love. The Princess came in a Golden coach, wearing a wonderful dress and slippers made of glass. How would Cinderella get anything like that?

Baroness I don't know—but I intend to find out. (*She glares*) And in any case—if it wasn't that scruffy little ragamuffin of yours, why are you looking so *guilty*? Now move—and if she's not there waiting . . .

The Baroness marches off in a temper

Baron (*following*) Medusa—wait . . .

The Baron exits

Asphyxia (*giggling*) Ooooh. We're all on our own.

Euthanasia With two men. (*She simpers*)

Men (*backing away*) Good night, girls.

Asphyxia Oh, don't go. The night is young, and I'm so beautiful.

Euthanasia Come to your little passion flower. (*She advances on Ammer*)

Ammer I'm sorry. I can't stand passion flowers. I get hay fever.

Asphyxia (*grabbing Tongs*) Come back to my boudoir with me, and I'll show you my *pièce de resistance.*

Tongs (*nervously*) Eh?

Asphyxia It's a great big barber's pole fixed over my fireplace.

Tongs What's that for?

Asphyxia To remind me how many close shaves I've had. (*She giggles*)

Euthanasia It's a pity you didn't remember to have one this morning. Your beard's coming through. (*She hurls herself at Ammer*) Stick with me, kiddo. I'll show you what a *real* woman's made of.

Ammer Help.

SONG 14 (*Asphyxia, Euthanasia, Ammer and Tongs*)

At the end of the song the Sisters sling Ammer and Tongs over their shoulders and carry them off

The Lights fade, then come up again at once

Dandini and a footman enter, the latter carrying the slipper on the cushion. Various characters meet him in a cross-over and try on the slipper without success. As the last person exits, Dandini and the Footman go

Music plays softly throughout this sequence

SONG 15

SCENE 4

The Kitchen of Stoneybroke Mansion

The room has been tidied. Cinders sits by the fire on a small stool, day-dreaming. The Baron and Baroness enter. She jumps to her feet

Baron (*to the Baroness*) You see. I told you she'd be here. (*He goes to Cinders in relief*)

Cinders What's the matter, Daddy?

Baroness (*fuming*) Nothing. (*She looks around*) Look at the state of this kitchen. It's an absolute disgrace. Tidy it up at once and make us some supper. I'm going to get changed.

The Baroness exits in a temper

Baron I've brought something back for you, Cinders. (*He gives her a small package*) It's a piece of cake.

Cinders Oh—er, thank you. (*She takes it*) Thank you, Daddy. (*She kisses him*)

Baron (*uncomfortably*) Er—Cinders . . .?

Cinders Yes?

Baron Were you . . .? I mean—did you . . .? Oh, never mind.

Cinders Never mind what?

Baron (*laughing shamefaced*) Well—I thought I saw you at the Ball tonight. Silly, isn't it?

Cinders (*turning away*) Yes. It is. (*She laughs nervously*)

Baron Anyway, you'd better try to tidy things up before your stepmother gets back. I'll go and change then I'll come back and help you with the supper.

The Baron exits

Cinders Poor Daddy. He's so kind to me. Oh, if only I could tell him the truth. (*She waltzes around, singing the waltz music from the Ball*)

Asphyxia and Euthanasia enter

Cinders almost collides with them

Oh . . .

Asphyxia And what's the matter with *you*?

Euthanasia Sly little cat.

Asphyxia (*pushing Cinders*) Take that.

Euthanasia And that. (*She pushes her again*)

Cinders (*bewildered*) What have I done?

Asphyxia I'll tell you what you've done, you cross-eyed little toad. You look like the Princess, that's what you've done.

Euthanasia Ferret faced little creep.

Cinders (*with spirit*) And why shouldn't I look like the Princess?

Asphyxia Because you're nothing but a scruffy little kitchenmaid, that's why.

Euthanasia *And* you haven't any manners.

Asphyxia *And* you're uglier than *she* is. (*She indicates her sister*)

Euthanasia *And* you're uglier than *I* . . . (*To Asphyxia*) Here—what do you mean, she's uglier than I am?

Asphyxia Well, dear—it's one of the penalties of age. You can't keep your looks forever, can you? I mean—look at you. You've got a face like a squeezed orange.

Euthanasia That's a lie. I've got the face of a saint.

Asphyxia Yes. A St Bernard.

Cinders giggles nervously

Euthanasia (*sharply*) And what are you sniggering at, bigmouth?

Cinders Nothing.

Buttons enters

Asphyxia (*to Cinders*) Well how about laughing *this* one off? (*She lifts her hand to hit her*)

Buttons (*quickly*) Hey—guess what.

The Sisters swing round to see him

Cinders (*running past them to join him*) Buttons.

Buttons (*holding on to her*) Prince Charming and that Dandini feller have just arrived in the village again. They're looking for a woman.

Asphyxia (*quickly*) Send them up here. I'm waiting.

Euthanasia He said a woman. Not a nervous breakdown.

Cinders (*eagerly*) Who is it they want, Buttons?

Buttons I dunno—but I did hear that the Prince fell in love with a beautiful woman at the Ball tonight, but she ran away and left him. Nobody knows who she was, but she dropped her glass slipper on the stairs, and the Prince says that whoever it fits, he's going to marry her.

All Marry her?

Buttons (*to Cinders*) Here—it wasn't . . .

Cinders quickly shushes him

I mean . . . Oh.

Asphyxia (*swooning*) Oh, my shoe. He found my shoe. I knew I'd left it somewhere.

Euthanasia What do you mean, *your* shoe? It's my shoe he's got. I distinctly remember it falling off as we ran up the stairs.

Asphyxia That wasn't your shoe you dropped, ducky—that was your teeth. It's *my* shoe. I tell you.

Euthanasia No it *isn't*. You couldn't get your shoes on, remember. *You* had to wear the *boxes*. It's *mine*.

Asphyxia *Tisn't*.

Euthanasia *Tis*.

The Sisters exit, arguing wildly with each other

Cinders Oh, Buttons. It isn't true, is it?

Buttons Course it is. I told you. (*Slight pause*) I—er—I suppose it *is* yours, Cinders. That glass slipper?

Cinders (*nodding*) I remember it falling off as I ran.

Buttons (*turning away*) So—I expect you'll be marrying the Prince now—won't you?

Cinders (*excitedly*) Oh, yes. Oh, Buttons—I'm so happy. I never dreamed that anything like this could happen to *me*.

Buttons (*downcast*) I see . . . (*He moves further away*)

Cinders (*not noticing*) I'll have fine clothes to wear, and servants to help me, and I can pay off all Daddy's debts, and then I'll . . . (*She notices him at last*) Buttons! What's the matter?

Buttons I'm—going.

Cinders *Going?* But where? Why?

Buttons Well—you won't want me, now, will you?

Cinders (*hurrying to him*) But I will, Buttons, I *will*. Oh, please don't go away *now*. Not when I'm so happy.

Buttons Why shouldn't I? You've got your Prince to look after you from now on. You won't need *me*.

Cinders But I will. More than ever.

Buttons Tara, Cinders.

Buttons hurries out, trying not to cry

Cinders (*calling*) Buttons—come back. You can come to the Castle *with* me.

The Baroness enters behind Cinders

You can be my own special pageboy. Oh, Buttons—come back. If it hadn't been for you, I'd never have *been* the Princess Crystal.

Baroness (*furiously*) So I was right. Cinderella *was* the Princess. I must warn my precious darlings at once.

The Baroness exits quickly

Cinders (*sobbing*) Buttons . . .

The Baron enters

Baron Cinderella. What is it?

Cinders Oh, Daddy! It's Buttons. He's gone away and left us. He thinks we won't be needing him any longer.

Baron Nonsense. Of course we shall. Now don't worry, my dear . . . *I'll* go and get him back.

The Baron exits. The Baroness enters, with the Sisters

Baroness (*sweetly*) Ahh, Cinderella, my own sweet little stepdaughter. Mumsy has a teeny-weeny job for you.

Cinders (*startled*) Pardon?

Asphyxia Wash your great lugholes out, you dozy little . . . I mean—(*sickly sweet*)—Mumsy has a little surprise for her very *favourite* daughter. (*To the Baroness*) Haven't you, Mummy?

Baroness Come to Mummy, *darling* one. (*She smiles evilly*)
Cinders (*frightened*) Why?
Euthanasia (*leering*) We want you to do something for us, *dearest*.
Baroness So come along. (*She crooks her finger*) Be a good girl.
Cinders (*backing away as they advance on her*) No.
Asphyxia (*grabbing her arm*) Stand still, or I'll break your arm.
Euthanasia To the attic with her. (*She grabs her other arm*)
Baroness Quickly, before the Prince arrives.
Cinders (*calling*) Help. Help. (*She struggles as she is dragged*)
Asphyxia It's no use screaming for help, *Princess.*
Euthanasia 'Cos no-one can hear you, *Princess.*
Baroness And if anybody's going to get the Prince, we'll make quite sure
it isn't *you*. Away with her.

*Calling for help, Cinders is dragged off by the Sisters, and the Baroness
follows behind*

A front cloth descends, depicting a quiet street

Buttons enters

Buttons (*wiping his eyes*) She can marry her rotten old Prince. See if *I* care.
(*He scuffs his shoes*) There's plenty of *other* girls who'd like to marry a
handsome, intelligent, witty and kindhearted feller like me, isn't there,
kids? Course there is. I could marry anybody I pleased, I could. Trouble
is—I don't seem to please anybody. I'm just Buttons, I am. Common old
Buttons. Never wanted unless there's any work to be done. I'm about as
much use as an Elastoplast on a wooden leg. (*He sits dejectedly*) Anyway
—why should *I* worry about her marrying that Prince Charming? Just
wait till she finds out that he beats her twice a day and locks her in the
Castle dungeons so she can't have any friends. Yes. Just you wait. She'll
come running to me and she'll say . . .

The Fairy Godmother enters

Fairy Godmother Buttons.
Buttons That's right. She'll say "Buttons" . . .
Fairy Godmother I need your help.
Buttons "I need your help." And *I'll* say . . .
Fairy Godmother (*firmly*) *Buttons.*
Buttons (*puzzled*) Eh? (*He turns*) Oh, it's her again. Fairy Liquid.
Fairy Godmother You must return to the Mansion at once. Cinderella
needs your help desperately.
Buttons No she doesn't. She's got her mouldy old Prince, now.
Fairy Godmother If you don't return to help her, she'll never marry the
Prince. Her wicked stepmother and stepsisters have locked her in an
attic room so that when the Prince calls, she will be unable to try on the
slipper of crystal.
Buttons (*shrugging*) Why should I care? It's me that loves Cinders not
him. If he goes away without finding her, she might decide to marry me,
after all.

Fairy Godmother Buttons. Listen to me. If you *truly* love Cinderella, then
you'll hasten to her aid. Think well. *Her* happiness rests in *your* hands.
If you are half the man I think you are, you will hurt yourself to make
her eternally happy. Do you understand?

Buttons (*wavering*) I *can't*—I mean . . . You didn't ought to ask me . . .
I . . . (*He decides*) Hang on, Cinders. *I'm coming.*

Buttons dashes off

Fairy Godmother (*to the audience*) Poor Buttons. He's so in love with
Cinderella, and yet it is written that she shall marry another. Still—by
this deed he will prove to himself and everyone else that he is no longer
a little boy, but a *man*. It would have been a simple task for *me* to set
Cinderella free in time to try on the slipper, but this way, Buttons and
she will be re-united as friends again. And now we must return to the
Mansion and see what happens. (*She waves her wand*)

The Fairy Godmother exits

The cloth flies up, revealing the kitchen

The Baroness hurries in breathlessly

Baroness Quickly. They're coming up the path.

Asphyxia enters, followed by Euthanasia

Asphyxia I'll let them in.

Euthanasia No. I'll do it. We don't want your face to frighten them away.

There is a knock on the door

All It's them.

They all rush for the door and collide

Dandini, the Prince and the Footman enter

Baroness (*recovering herself*) Your Highnessship. (*She curtsies*)

Asphyxia (*gaping at the slipper*) Oh—what are you doing with my slipper?

Prince (*aghast*) *Your* slipper?

Euthanasia (*sweetly*) Ignore her, darling. It's quite obvious that such a
dainty little slipper belongs to *me*.

Dandini Perhaps we should settle the argument by letting you try it on?

Asphyxia She's *always* trying it on.

Euthanasia Listen who's talking. The walking bear trap. (*To Dandini*)
Hand it over.

Asphyxia Not so fast, Madame là Mode. I'm first in line.

Euthanasia You certainly were when it came to handing mouths out.

Asphyxia Oh, go stick your head in the mincing-machine. It might im-
prove your looks.

Prince (*signalling*) Footman.

Baroness (*beaming*) *I* know why they call him a *footman*.

Dandini Really?

Baroness Yes. It's because he's *carrying the slipper*. (*She chortles with laughter*)
Prince (*wearily*) Well—who is to be first?
Sister Me.
Baroness Asphyxia, I think—

Asphyxia smirks with triumph

—will wait till last.

Asphyxia scowls as her sister smirks

Euthanasia I'll sit on this chair. (*She gets a chair*)
Asphyxia Careful. They'll only support up to half a ton.

Euthanasia scowls and slips off her shoe. The Footman kneels and tries to force on the slipper

Euthanasia Push. PUSH! (*She screams with pain*) Owwww!
Footman I'm afraid your foot is too large, Madam.
Euthanasia Rubbish. It's the slipper that's too small. Bring me a larger size.
Dandini I'm sorry. It's this one or nothing.
Euthanasia Wait—I'll take my sock off.

With the help of the others, she takes off several yards of multi-coloured stocking

Now where's that slipper again?

Once more they attempt to force it on

Owwww!
Dandini It's quite obvious that the slipper is not going to fit. Let the other one try, now.
Asphyxia (*dragging her sister off the chair*) Out of the way, fatness. Make room for the future Princess.

The Footman slips on the shoe

It fits. It fits. (*She displays it*)
Prince What?
Dandini But it can't do.

They gaze in horror at Asphyxia

Buttons comes flying in

Buttons (*spotting them*) Oooh . . .!

Buttons careers round and exits again

Asphyxia (*triumphantly*) Bring out the crown. Start writing the invitations.
Baroness Oh, my precious. (*She runs to embrace her*)
Euthanasia (*snarling*) Just a minute. Just a minute. (*She pushes the Baroness out of the way and stands next to Asphyxia*) I think there's

something fishy going on here. (*She pulls at the leg and it comes away in her hands. It is a false one*) Aha! (*She waves the leg*) I knew it wasn't hers. She's got so many varicose veins in her legs, the last time *she* went to a fancy dress ball, she won first prize as a road map.

Prince (*relieved*) Saved. (*He mops his brow*)

Dandini (*icily*) And now we'll try the slipper on your *real* foot. (*He fits it himself*) Impossible.

Asphyxia Wait—there's something stopping my foot from going right in.

Euthanasia Yes. They're called *toes*.

Baroness Don't worry, my sweet. Mummy will fix it.

The Baroness dashes off

Prince Come, Dandini.

Dandini places the slipper back on the cushion and they prepare to leave

The Baroness enters waving a huge axe

Baroness (*to Asphyxia*) Quickly, darling. Hold out your foot.

Asphyxia (*leaping up with a shriek*) Keep away from me! Help! (*She races round the kitchen pursued by the Baroness*) Help!

Baroness (*calling*) No, no, poppet. It's for your own good. It won't hurt for long.

Asphyxia dashes off, pursued by the Baroness and Euthanasia

Prince Well, Dandini—that looks like that. We've tried the slipper on everyone in the land, but it seems to fit no-one. Our search is hopeless. We'd better return to the Castle.

Dandini One moment, Your Highness. Didn't you once say that you were under the impression that Baron Hardupp had *three* daughters?

Prince (*remembering*) Of course. The young girl in the woods. Dandini. Is it possible . . .?

The Baroness and Euthanasia race in, still chasing a screaming Asphyxia

Baroness (*stopping and curtsying*) Won't keep you a minute.

Asphyxia (*yelling*) Save me! Help!

Prince (*sternly*) Madam. Haven't you *three* daughters?

Asphyxia and Euthanasia stop running in shock

Baroness ⎱ Three daughters? Oh, no. Only *one.* ⎱ (*Speaking together*)
Sisters ⎰   ⎰

Asphyxia ⎱ *Me.* ⎱ (*Speaking together*)
Euthanasia ⎰   ⎰

Baroness These two.

Prince Oh. (*His shoulders slump*)

The Prince, Dandini and the Footman turn to go

Buttons dashes in with Cinders

Buttons Hey—stop. Wait. (*He pulls Cinders forwards*)

Baroness ⎫
Sisters ⎰ *(in horror)* Cinderella. ⎱ *(Speaking together)*

Prince *(seeing her)* Cinderella.

Dandini *(to the Baroness sternly)* I thought you said there were no other daughters?

Baroness *(trying to bluster)* There isn't—she's just a—a—a *kitchenmaid.*

Buttons Oh no, she isn't. *(To the audience)* Is she, kids? *(To the Prince)* This is Baron Hardupp's *real* daughter, Cinderella.

Prince *(excitedly)* It's *her*, Dandini. I *know* it is.

Dandini We'll soon see when she tries the slipper on. Come, Cinderella. There's nothing to be afraid of.

Dandini escorts Cinders to the chair and she sits. The Footman moves towards her with the cushion and the slipper

Asphyxia ⎫
Euthanasia ⎰ *(wailing)* Oh Mummykins. It's going to fit her. ⎱ *(Speaking together)*

The Baroness quickly sticks her leg out and trips the Footman. He staggers, and the slipper flies off into the wings

Buttons *(aghast)* The slipper.

Dandini *(looking off)* It's shattered into a thousand pieces.

Baroness *(smirking)* How unfortunate.

Asphyxia Now she won't be able to try it on.

Euthanasia Poor thing.

Buttons But it *was* Cinderella's slipper. It *was.*

Dandini But how can we be sure?

Cinders Wait.

Cinders gets up and dashes off

Asphyxia Where's she going?

Euthanasia She'll never join *that* together with Uhu.

Baroness She's coming back.

Cinders enters with the other slipper

Cinders Look. Here's the *other* slipper. *(Holds it up to show them)*

Prince It's identical.

Cinders slips it on

And it fits. *(Triumphantly)* My search is over. Cinderella, I claim you as my bride.

Cinderella stands. The Prince embraces her

The Baron, Ammer and Tongs enter

Baron What's going on?

Baroness *(snivelling)* Cinderella's going to marry the Prince, and we're all going to be punished for all the nasty things we've been doing to her. *(She sobs)*

Buttons And it jolly well serves you right—(*to the audience*)—doesn't it, kids?

The Sisters cling together unhappily

Cinders (*going to the Baroness*) Don't cry, Mother.
Baroness (*stopping sobbing in shock*) Eh? *What* did you say?
Cinders I said "Don't cry, Mother". I gladly forgive you for everything you did; for how can I bear to see someone so unhappy when I'm so wonderfully happy myself.
Baroness Oh, Cinders. (*She embraces her*)
Cinders (*turning to Buttons*) And as for Buttons. My own, darling Buttons. You shall be my own special pageboy, and anything you want will be yours for the asking.
Buttons Cor—smashing.
Prince But what about *those* two? (*He indicates the Sisters*)
Dandini What are we going to do about *them*?

The Sisters drop to their knees

Asphyxia Oh, mercy. Mercy.
Euthanasia We were only so nasty because we were jealous of you.
Asphyxia You were so beautiful and we're so ugly. We thought we'd *never* get married if the boys saw you first.
Euthanasia We're so sorry. (*She sobs*) Please forgive us.
Cinders Of *course* I forgive you.
Asphyxia Don't have us executed.
Euthanasia Or thrown into jail.
Cinders I forgive you.
Asphyxia Please don't banish us.
Euthanasia Or send us to Butlins.
Cinders (*louder*) I *forgive* you.
Asphyxia (*looking up*) We heard you the *first* time, dearie, but this is our last chance to pick up an Award for the Best Supporting Actress.

The Sisters scramble to their feet as the Baron steps forward, joyfully

Baron So everything's worked out all right at last, and my little Cinderella will no longer be a poor Baron's daughter, but the wife of Prince Charming.
Baroness And just to show how sorry we are for all the evil things we did, I and my daughters will write out all the Wedding Invitations.
Prince Splendid.
Asphyxia Well, all right. But before we begin, *we've* got a little invitation of our own to send out, haven't we, Euthie?
Euthanasia You mean . . .? (*She indicates Ammer and Tongs with her head*)
Ammer (*spotting it*) Oooer. Excuse us. (*He backs away*)
Tongs We have to collect the Prime Minister's furniture from Number Ten. (*He edges away*)

Ammer and Tongs turn and run for their lives

Asphyxia } (*calling*) Wait. Come back. } (*Speaking together*)
Euthanasia }

The Sisters pick up their skirts and chase off after them

Buttons Tally-ho!

The Fairy Godmother enters

Fairy Godmother So, Cinderella—your Prince has found you at last, and
I grant you *both* the gift of eternal happiness. The broken slipper will be
restored to you, and from this moment on the story of your love will
pass into legend and your names be remembered forever.
   And now to the Castle you must away—
   To prepare the joyous Wedding Day.

SONG 15

As the song ends—

the CURTAIN *falls*

SCENE 5

SONG SHEET, or as required

SCENE 6

The Ballroom of Castle Glamorous

FINALE:
Sunbeams
Junior Misses
Chorus
Major Domo
Fairy Godmother
Ammer and Tongs
Baron and Baroness
Dandini
Asphyxia and Euthanasia
Buttons
Cinderella and Prince Charming

CURTAIN

FURNITURE AND PROPERTY LIST

ACT I

SCENE 1

On stage: High brick wall with iron gates

Off stage: Envelope with letter **(Buttons)**
Small suitcase **(Baron)**
Pile of gift-wrapped packages **(Footmen)**
Chair **(Ammer)**

Personal: **Asphyxia:** handbag
Euthanasia: handbag

SCENE 2

On stage: Scattered sticks and twigs

Off stage: Bundle of sticks **(Cinders)**

Personal: **Buttons:** handkerchief with hole in it

SCENE 3

On stage: Tree stumps
Sticks and twigs

Off stage: Rabbits with price marks **(Prince, Huntsmen)**
Bundle of sticks **(Cinders)**
Bundle of sticks **(Buttons)**

Personal: **Fairy Godmother:** staff, wand, silver star
Prince: invitation tickets

SCENE 4

Off stage: Candles **(Dancers)**

SCENE 5

On stage: Large brick fireplace, with kettle on hob
Scrubbed kitchen table. *On it:* tablecloth
Clothes-horse. *On it:* towel
Pail and wash-cloth on floor (for **Cinders**)

Off stage: Pumpkin, 6 white mice, 2 lizards **(Cinders)**
Pair of crystal slippers **(Cinders)**
Golden coach **(Children)**
Stardust **(Fairy Godmother)**

Personal: **Baron:** 4 invitation tickets

ACT II

Scene 1

Personal: **Baroness:** invitation ticket
Ammer: invitation ticket
Tongs: invitation ticket
Guests: invitation tickets
Asphyxia: invitation ticket
Buttons: invitation ticket

Scene 2

On stage: Large clock above staircase: hands at 9.15—changed during action

Off stage: Glasses **(Guests)**
Trays of champagne glasses **(Footmen)**
Knives and forks **(Asphyxia)**
Spoons **(Euthanasia)**
Spare glass slipper **(Footman)**
Silk cushion **(Footman)**

Personal: **Major Domo:** staff

Scene 4a

On stage: As Act I, Scene 5, but tidied
Add 1 small stool by fire

Scene 4b

On stage: Small seat or stool

Scene 4c

On stage: As Scene 4a

Off stage: Trick wooden leg **(Asphyxia)**
Axe **(Baroness)**
Crystal slipper **(Cinders)**

LIGHTING PLOT

Property fittings required: kitchen fire effect, chandelier (optional)
Several simple internal and external sets

ACT I

To open: Full exterior daylight, bright and sunny

Cue 1   As SCENE 1 ends   (Page 10)
          Cross-fade to front-cloth lighting

Cue 2   As SCENE 2 ends   (Page 12)
          Cross-fade to woodland glade lighting, day

Cue 3   As SCENE 3 ends   (Page 22)
          Cross-fade to front-cloth lighting, day

Cue 4   As SCENE 4 ends   (Page 22)
          Cross-fade to interior lighting, kitchen

Cue 5   **Buttons:** "Off to the Ball", **Cinders:** "Yes."   (Page 29)
          Fade overall lighting and fire to low

Cue 6   **Buttons** exits   (Page 30)
          Further fade of overall lighting

Cue 7   **Fairy Godmother:** ". . . arrange for your ball gown."   (Page 31)
          Bring up lighting effect on **Fairies**

Cue 8   **Fairy Godmother:** "And now for the coach."   (Page 32)
          Block-out, flash, Lights up to golden brightness

ACT II

To open: Front-cloth lighting, evening

Cue 9   At close of SCENE 1   (Page 36)
          Cross-fade to brilliant ballroom lighting, with (optional)
          chandelier

Cue 10 As waltz starts   (Page 39)
          Fade almost to Black-out, pause, return to full

Cue 11 As **Sisters** entertain   (Page 42)
          Fade to spots on **Sisters***: as entertainment finishes return to
          full*

Cue 12 **Prince:** ". . . start to come alive."   (Page 43)
          Coloured lights on dancers: return to normal as **Cinders** *flees*

Cue 13 At end of SCENE 2   (Page 44)
          Cross-fade to front-cloth, night

EFFECTS PLOT

ACT I

Cue 1   As **Cinders** enters in SCENE 2   (Page 11)
            Birdsong

ACT II

Cue 2   As clock hands move to midnight   (Page 43)
            Twelve o'clock strikes

MADE AND PRINTED IN GREAT BRITAIN BY
LATIMER TREND & COMPANY LTD PLYMOUTH